NEGROES, BALLOTS, AND JUDGES

NEGROES,

BALLOTS,

AND

JUDGES

National Voting Rights Legislation
in the Federal Courts

by Donald S. Strong

Published for the Bureau of Public
Administration, University of Alabama

by

UNIVERSITY OF ALABAMA PRESS

University, Alabama

340
St 8 n
68 4 76
January 1970

Manufactured in the United States of America

Foreword

Professor Donald S. Strong has made earlier studies of Negro voting over the last twenty years. Soon after *Smith v. Allwright* outlawed the Texas white primary, he examined the impact of the case in "The Rise of Negro Voting in Texas."[1] His *Registration of Voters in Alabama*,[2] while treating all aspects of registration, dealt at some length with Negro voting and the obstacles thereto. Shortly thereafter he published an article, "The Future of the Negro Voter in the South," in the *Journal of Negro Education*.[3] Thus Professor Strong is no newcomer to the analysis of registration and voting in the South.

A decade after the *Allwright* case, more than a million Negroes were voting in some areas of the South, but in others Negroes desiring to register and to vote met unyielding resistance. In an effort to overcome this opposition, Congress passed the Civil Rights Acts of 1957 and 1960. It was soon apparent that much resistance to these laws centered in the states of Louisiana, Mississippi, and Alabama, and it was in them that most litigation arose. It is on the federal court decisions in these states that the author focuses his attention. Any act of Congress acquires its meaning through judicial interpretation. Yet all litigation under the civil rights laws involved equity proceedings, and in court actions without a

[1]*American Political Science Review*, 42 (1948), 510-522.
[2]Bureau of Public Administration, University, Alabama (1956).
[3]Vol. 26 (1957), 400-407.

jury the role of the judge is of peculiar importance. Hence the appropriateness of the title: *Negroes, Ballots, and Judges.* All federal voting rights legislation prior to the act of 1965 was at best a very qualified success. With the passage of years this legislation became more effective; but if evaluated in terms of the increase in the number of Negroes registered, these laws produced rather disappointing results. This is the burden of the author's argument in Chapters I and II. In Chapter III, he explores the reasons for these modest accomplishments. He notes that the legislatures in all three states were concerned with rendering federal legislation ineffective. Moreover, a federal judge in the South often encounters a conflict between the regional values that he espouses and his role as a member of the federal judiciary. In a brief epilogue, the author examines the Voting Rights Act of 1965 and finds in it an infinitely more dramatic use of federal power.

This study was made possible by grants from the University of Alabama Research Committee and the Bureau of Public Administration. Professor Strong acknowledges his gratitude to both of these agencies.

ROBERT B. HIGHSAW
*Director of the Bureau of
Public Administration
University of Alabama*

Table of Contents

I

Legislative History

IN THE HISTORY of the struggle for the ballot by the southern Negro, the period 1957-1965 is unique. The year 1957 ended the period when the role of the federal government was limited to keeping the courts open to private Negro litigants. The Fifteenth Amendment provides "The right of citizens . . . to vote shall not be denied or abridged . . . by any State on account of race, color, or previous condition of servitude." Yet an individual Negro had to hire a lawyer to institute a civil suit to vindicate this right. In 1957 Congress rediscovered and dusted off Section 2 of the Fifteenth Amendment: "The Congress shall have power to enforce this article by appropriate legislation." The Civil Rights Acts of 1957, 1960, and 1964—all appropriate legislation—ended the earlier neutrality of the federal government and gave it the affirmative responsibility of aiding Negroes whose voting rights were being denied or abridged. Cases would now be named *U.S. v. X.* The Voting Rights Act of 1965 ended the era. An exasperated Congress passed a much more drastic act that took the responsibility for Negro enfranchisement out of the hands of the courts and gave it to the executive. The three earlier acts achieved only limited results in ending Negro disfranchisement but produced a large amount of litigation. This study chronicles this litigation, discusses the problems of enforcing the acts, and suggests reasons for the modest success of this approach.

Prior to the Supreme Court's decision in *Smith v. Allwright*[1] in 1944, any voting by Negroes in the 11 states of the former Confederacy was exceptional. The *Allwright* decision dealt a mortal blow to the white primary, which from the segregationist standpoint was the ideal device for Negro disfranchisement. It disfranchised no whites yet categorically excluded all Negroes from the Democratic primary, the only important election. In the following 13 years the number of Negroes registered to vote rose from a quarter of a million to a million and a half.[2] This increased participation was not uniform throughout the South. The greatest increases occurred in counties with a relatively low percentage of Negroes. In most counties in the 11 Confederate states, Negroes encountered relatively few obstacles to registration and voting. Negro voting might be accepted as a necessary evil, but it was accepted. Resistance to Negro political participation was intense only in a region within a region. Counties with a high percentage of Negroes—the black belt or old plantation areas—were the centers of resistance to Negro voting.[3] Although some futile last-ditch efforts were made to retain the white primary, the foes of Negro voting now turned to the registration process as their chief weapon. It would make no difference if Negroes were theoretically free to vote in the Democratic primary if they could not even register. The problem to which the three civil rights acts were directed was the registration of Negroes in counties of Negro concentration.

The Civil Rights Act of 1957 is historically significant because it was the first time in three-quarters of a century that Congress passed a law governing race relations. Al-

---

[1]321 U.S. 649 (1944).
[2]D. Matthews and J. Prothro, *Negroes and the New Southern Politics* (New York: Harcourt, Brace, 1966), p. 18.
[3]*Ibid.*, pp. 115-135.

though history-making in this respect, the law was in all other respects cautious and tentative. The act created the Civil Rights Commission and gave new powers to the Department of Justice. The Commission is an independent agency with investigatory functions only. It collects information in several areas, but with respect to voting, it is required to

> investigate allegations in writing . . . that certain citizens of the United States are being deprived of their right to vote . . . by reason of their color, race, religion, or national origin . . .

The Commission investigates and reports to the President and to the Congress; it has no power to prosecute.

The additional powers given the Department of Justice are an amendment to Section 2004 of the Revised Statutes (42 U.S.C. 1971). This section provides that:

> All citizens of the United States who are otherwise qualified by law to vote at any election by the people in any state . . . county, city . . . shall be entitled . . . to vote at all such elections without distinction of race, color, or previous condition of servitude; any constitution, law, custom, usage, or regulation of any state . . . to the contrary notwithstanding.

The amendment reads, in part:

> No person, whether acting under color of law or otherwise, shall intimidate, threaten, or coerce . . . any other person for the purpose of interfering with the right of such person to vote or to vote as he may choose . . . for [any federal official].

Even more of an innovation is the power given the Attorney General to intervene at public expense on behalf of persons whose right to vote is threatened. The act provides:

> Whenever any person has engaged or there are reasonable grounds to believe that any person is about to engage in any act or practice which would deprive any other person of any right or privilege secured by subsection (a) or (b),

> the Attorney General may institute for the United States
> . . . a civil action or other proceedings for preventive relief,
> including an application for a permanent or temporary in-
> junction, restraining order, or other order. In any proceeding
> hereunder the United States shall be liable for costs the
> same as a private person.

The act provides, further, that the United States may take
jurisdiction regardless of whether the party has exhausted
his administrative remedies under state law. This provision
is designed to eliminate the fantastic legal delaying actions
formerly inflicted on Negro litigants before their cause could
be tried on its merits.

Another innovation of the law was its reliance on civil
procedure. The stress on civil procedure stemmed from a
lack of faith in southern juries. Congress feared that if
the criminal-law approach were taken, juries would not convict violators of an unpopular law. With the emphasis on
civil actions, southern election officers need have no fear of
the federal penitentiary. In fact, a registrar of voters or other
local official would have to go to considerable trouble to
get himself jailed. Imprisonment or fine could result from
civil contempt (for instance, a refusal to comply with a court
order) but a person could regain his freedom by merely re-
considering his refusal and complying with the order. Getting
oneself in jail for criminal contempt would be even more
difficult. This would require committing an action that a
federal judge had specifically prohibited. Conceivably a
local official might be enjoined from doing bodily harm to
Negroes attempting to register. Should he then assault a
Negro attempting to register, he could be punished for criminal
contempt and given a fixed sentence. However, he could
demand a jury trial if the prison sentence were in excess of
45 days or the fine over $300.

The history of the Civil Rights Act from 1957 to 1960 is
chiefly a tale of frustration. During the three years prior
to the 1960 amendments, the Justice Department filed only

four suits. In the first case, *U.S. v. Raines*,[4] a district court held the act unconstitutional, and it was not until February, 1960, that the U.S. Supreme Court upheld the constitutionality of the legislation.[5] In *U.S. v. Alabama*,[6] the Macon County case, the three county registrars had resigned, and the district court stated that the act did not authorize the Justice Department to sue a state. The other two cases had somewhat happier results. In *U.S. v. Fayette County Democratic Executive Committee*[7] the Justice Department succeeded in having the defendants enjoined from operating a white primary within the Democratic Party in that Tennessee county. Although the white primary had been invalidated sixteen years earlier, it is probable that no Negro in Fayette County was in a position financially or otherwise to institute a private suit. The Government won in a case arising in Louisiana, *U.S. v. McElveen*.[8] This suit attacked the validity of a purge from the voter registration rolls of Negro voters, but not of white voters similarly situated. The Government's evidence showed that 1,377 Negro voters and only 10 white voters were removed from the voter registration rolls for alleged deficiencies in their original application forms. The court found that at least 50 per cent of the unchallenged applications of white voters had the same defects and deficiencies and ordered the purged Negroes to be restored to the rolls. Thus, in its first 33 months of operation the Civil Rights Act of 1957 had made no significant changes in the custom of Negro disfranchisement.

Although our concern here is the activity of the Justice Department, not that of the Civil Rights Commission, one incident in the Commission's experience illustrates clearly the attitude of local and state officials with whom the Department of Justice had to deal. In December, 1958, and

4172 F. Supp. 552 (1959).
5362 U.S. 17 (1960).
6171 F. Supp. 720 (1959).
7V (1960) *Race Relations Law Reporter* 421. Hereinafter cited as *RRLR*.
8180 F. Supp. 10 (1960).

January, 1959, the Commission held public hearings in Montgomery, Alabama. The hearings produced a mountain of evidence that Negroes were being discriminated against in registration. However, Attorney General Patterson (then governor-elect) made every effort to frustrate the Commission's activities. On his advice, the Macon County registrars took refuge in the Fifth Amendment and refused to testify or produce any records. An instructive incident occurred toward the close of the hearing when Commissioner Battle, former governor of Virginia, addressed the uncooperative Macon registrars. After reminding the registrars that his forebears were born in Alabama and assuring them of his affection for the state, he attempted to reason with them:

> The majority of the members of the next Congress will not be sympathetic toward the South, and punitive legislation may be passed, and this hearing may be used in the advocacy of that legislation, which will react adversely . . . to you in Alabama.
>
> . . . may I say to you and as one who is tremendously interested in the southern cause; will you kindly reevaluate the situation and see if there is not some way you . . . may cooperate a little more fully with this Commission and not have it said by our enemies in Congress that the people of Alabama were not willing to explain their conduct when requested to do so?[9]

This eminently intelligent advice was ignored. Instead the Alabamians listened to the advice of Attorney General Patterson, who counseled:

> Our duty in this case is clear: We must do everything within our power to prevent this unlawful invasion of the state of Alabama's judicial officers by the legislative and executive arms of the Federal Government . . . In fights of this nature there can be no surrender of principle to expediency. The time for retreating has come to an end.[10]

[9]*With Liberty and Justice for All: An Abridgement of the Report of the U.S. Commission on Civil Rights*, 1959, pp. 69-70.
[10]*Ibid.*, p. 70.

Governor Battle's remarks were prophetic. The Civil Rights Act of 1960, based largely on the recommendations of the Commission on Civil Rights, was passed by an unsympathetic Congress. The new law[11] required election officials to preserve registration records for a period of 22 months from the date of any general, special, or primary election for a federal officer. Upon the demand of the Attorney General any such records must be made available for inspection or reproduction.[12] It provided, further, that if registrars resigned, the state itself could be made a defendant in a suit. The meaning of the word *vote* was clarified; it included "all action necessary to make a vote effective including, but not limited to, registration or other action required by state law prerequisite to voting . . ." The most important innovation was the pattern-or-practice provision. The 1957 act compelled the Government to proceed individual-by-individual. Consider a hypothetical county with 6,005 Negro adults, none of whom are registered. Five Negroes attempt to register, are turned down, and eventually win a suit under the 1957 law. The county now has five Negro voters and 6,000 who are not registered, many of the latter possessing the same qualifications as the former. In order to accelerate registration, the law permits the Attorney General to plead that many of the unregistered 6,000 are disfranchised as a result of a pattern or practice that has earlier disfranchised the five. The Attorney General must first win a suit under the 1957 act, that is, in our example he must first enfranchise the five. Thereafter, he may request the court to find that a "pattern or practice" of racial discrimination in voting exists in that county. If the court, after examining the

[11]Public Law 86-449, 86th Congress.

[12]The need for preventing the destruction of records is indicated by the "introduction of a bill in the Alabama Senate requiring registrars to destroy within 30 days the applications and questionnaires of rejected applicants for registration. The bill, which passed both houses by unanimous vote, was amended only to make destruction of the records permissive rather than mandatory." *With Liberty and Justice for All,* pp. 73-74.

evidence, rules that such a pattern or practice exists, any Negro resident shall be entitled to a court order declaring him qualified to vote upon proof that: (1) he is qualified to vote *under state law* and (2) he has since the finding of the court been deprived of the opportunity to register solely because of race or color. This provision contemplates that a district judge himself is to determine whether the prospective voter satisfied the standards of the *state* law. It is assumed that state laws will be nondiscriminatory on their face and that if applied by a federal judge will, in fact, be administered in a nondiscriminatory fashion.

Or a district judge has the option of appointing a referee who will decide whether applicants qualify under state law. Persons who, since the "pattern or practice" finding has been made by the court, have been rejected for registration on what they believe to be racial grounds may appear before the referee and demonstrate to his satisfaction their ability to meet the state voting requirement. Hearings held before the referee are *ex parte*. A list of the applicants he finds qualified under state law is submitted to the district judge, who must transmit this list to the state attorney general and to local election officials and order them to show cause within ten days why the court should not order the registration of the persons listed. If no protests from state or local officials are forthcoming, the court orders that the persons named in the referee's document be registered. If local registrars wish to contend that the denial of registration was made on nondiscriminatory grounds, they may appear in court and defend their decisions. The judge must then decide between the recommendations of the referee and the claims of the local officials. These officials are not defendants in a criminal proceeding; they risk no fine or jail sentence—only the possibility that the court may rule that they have, contrary to their claims, denied registration to a person solely because of race or color.

The 1960 law denied registrars such easy ways out as destroying the evidence or resigning from their jobs, and it empowered the courts to take judicial notice of what any layman knew—namely, that disfranchisement was the result of a pattern or practice.

The Civil Rights Act of 1964[13] was a major effort to strike down discrimination in many areas in American life. The sections relating to voting were only a minor aspect of the law, and most of these provisions merely put into statutory form ideas that the courts had formulated over the preceding four years. Registrars could not "apply any standard . . . different from the standards, . . . applied . . . to other individuals within the same county . . . who have been found by State officials to be qualified to vote," nor deny the right to vote because of any technical or inconsequential error in the registration form. Use of a literacy test was limited. To be permissible, a literacy test must be "administered to each individual and . . . conducted wholly in writing, and . . . a certified copy of the test and the answers given by the individual [must be] furnished to him within 25 days . . ." Another section attempted to speed up voting-rights litigation by requiring courts to give it high priority. The act was approved on July 2, 1964; the much more drastic Voting Rights Act of 1965 was passed 13 months later. Hence, there was not too much time for the voting section of the 1964 Civil Rights Act to have an effect. The history of litigation is largely a story of litigation under the 1960 law.

[13]Public Law 88-352, 88th Congress.

II

What Constitutes Intimidation, Threats, or Coercion

Laws DESIGNED TO enfranchise Negroes had to be interpreted and put into effect by federal district judges. This chapter attempts to set forth the interpretation given them—to explain what they came to mean when applied in actual situations. The Department of Justice filed a total of 71 cases,[1] but a great many of these were never brought to trial. Of those actually tried, many of the important ones were appealed before a case was finally disposed of. What follows is a statement of what the law was when the Voting Rights Act of 1965 made the earlier legislation obsolete.

COERCION

The Department of Justice classifies cases in terms of the two sections of the U.S. Code under which they arise. The prohibition on racial discrimination appears in 42 U.S.C. Section 1971 (a), whereas the ban on intimidation, threats, or coercion appears in Section 1971 (b). Threats or coercion

[1]U.S. Congress, House, Subcommittee No. 5, Committee on the Judiciary, *Hearings, Voting Rights,* 89th Congress, 1st Session, 1965, p. 5.

may take the form either of economic pressure or physical violence. Let us turn our attention first to cases involving economic coercion. An early case of this type was *U.S. v. Deal, et al.*[2] This involved retaliation by the merchants of East Carroll Parish, Louisiana, against a Negro farmer named Atlas, who had testified before the Civil Rights Commission about wholesale Negro disfranchisement in his parish. Acting in concert, they refused to gin his cotton or conduct ordinary business with him. After Justice Department intervention, the court issued a consent decree by which the boycotting merchants agreed to desist. Ginning of Mr. Atlas's cotton was resumed, but he still was not a registered voter. Overcoming discrimination at the registrar's office would call for a separate case. Atlas merely vindicated the right to call attention to his disfranchisement without economic retribution.

The cases of *U.S. v. Beaty, U.S. v. Barcroft,* and *U.S. v. Atkeison*[3] were well publicized. They arose in Haywood and Fayette Counties, two West Tennessee counties not far from Memphis. All three cases involved economic reprisal against Negroes who had recently registered. Although there were few legal obstacles to Negro registration in Tennessee prior to May, 1960, no Negroes were registered in Haywood County and only 58 in Fayette. Landowners sent eviction notices to all tenants and sharecroppers who had registered, and various merchants declined to do business with them. Defendants in the Haywood case were 50 private citizens and four corporations; in the Fayette case 80 private citizens and one bank. The cases were finally terminated in May and July, 1962, respectively, by a consent decree. The decree contained express prohibitions on terminating employment, evicting, or changing the customary terms of tenancy or refusing to lend money. As of January, 1963, approximately 2,000 Negroes were registered in Haywood County; in Fayette County the figure was approximately 3,000.

[2]VI (1961) *RRLR* 474.
[3]VI (1961) *RRLR* 201; VII (1962) 484.

A different aspect of economic coercion was alleged in the case of *U.S. v. Board of Education of Greene County*.[4] In this Mississippi county the United States brought action against the board of education, seeking a court order requiring defendants to re-hire a teacher who had participated in a voter registration campaign and law suit and whose one-year employment contract had not been renewed after its expiration. Her school principal recommended her re-employment, but the county superintendent had turned down the recommendation. There was introduced some conflicting testimony concerning the competence and "cooperativeness" of the business teacher, Mrs. Talbert. The Greene County superintendent of schools had the following to say concerning his reasons for not renewing her appointment: ". . . plus the fact that she was involved in litigation which was not conducive to good work from her nor for getting the best from the school nor good for the relations among teachers. It was a controversial matter."

The U.S. District Court for the Southern District of Mississippi dismissed the complaint, finding that the teacher had no vested right in a new contract. Under Mississippi law a board need give no reason for failing to re-hire teachers, and the court asserted that there was no convincing evidence that the board was motivated by the teacher's political activities. Here is a situation reminiscent of cases under the National Labor Relations Act, in which the National Labor Relations Board has to decide whether an employee has been fired for inefficiency, as the employer asserts, or whether the real cause of dismissal was the plaintiff's union membership. In the present case the district judge dismissed the Government's contention that failure to re-hire her would have the effect of intimidating other Negroes from applying to register to vote. The decision was upheld by the Fifth Circuit Court of Appeals.[5]

[4]VII (1962) *RRLR* 770.
[5]332 F. 2d 40 (1964).

Economic coercion was involved in a case arising in Wilcox County, Alabama, which had had no Negroes registered for over half a century. In the spring of 1963, a Negro insurance salesman named Lonnie Brown, who had lived in the county all his life save for a period in the armed services, assumed the leadership in a registration drive. On May 30, 1963, Brown received a registered letter signed by W. Henderson Bruce and 27 other landowners, telling him to stay off all land owned or rented by them. Brown had previously had free access to these properties to collect insurance premiums from tenants residing there. It was necessary for Brown's company to transfer him to another part of the state.

The Attorney General moved for an injunction against Bruce and the other landowners. Oral arguments on defendants' motion to dismiss the complaint were heard on April 7, 1964. District Judge Thomas granted the motion to dismiss but gave no reason for the dismissal. The Government appealed. In *U.S. v. Bruce, et al.*[6] the Court of Appeals overruled the district court and granted the injunction. The conduct of the defendants would have been perfectly legal if not colored with the bad intent of interfering with the right to vote. Defendants could not invoke the trespass law against ". . . Brown, who had previously been given free access to the property, as a . . . means of coercion for the purpose of interfering with his right or the rights of others whom he represented in exercising their right to register and vote."

Not all coercion is economic. The language of 1971(b) is broad:

> No person, whether acting under color of law or otherwise, shall intimidate, threaten, coerce . . . any other person for the purpose of interfering with the right of such person to vote. . . .

While the language is broad enough to cover intimidation by private parties, most cases have involved intimidation by

[6]353 F. 2d 474 (1965).

local officials by means of baseless arrests and the misuse of local law-enforcement. A truly amazing case, *U.S. v. Wood*,[7] involves state criminal prosecution of a victim of violence by a state official. John Hardy, a Tennessee Negro, had been conducting a registration school in Walthall County, Mississippi. He accompained two Negroes to the office of the registrar, who ordered him out of the office at gunpoint. As he was leaving, the registrar hit him over the head with a pistol, saying, "Get out of here you damn son of a bitch and don't come back in here." Shortly thereafter, the Negro, not the registrar, was arrested for disturbing the peace. One of his companions stated in an affadavit introduced at the trial, "John said, [to the sheriff] 'Will you allow me to tell my side of the story?' The sheriff said, 'Don't give me none of your head, boy, or I will beat you within an inch of your life'." U.S. District Judge Cox refused the Justice Department's request for an order halting the disturbing-the-peace prosecution. No "controlling question of law" was involved. The Court of Appeals overruled him and issued a temporary restraining order.[8] Apparently the appellate judges were persuaded by the Government's contention that this was an instance of intimidation that might deter other organizers from coming to the county in an effort to disturb the peaceful situation wherein none of the 2,490 Negroes of voting age in the county were registered. Although the Government won its case, no Negroes were thereby made voters. The only effect of the case was that Mississippi was compelled to drop prosecution of the victim of violence.

In other cases where the Justice Department sues to restrain misuse of state criminal procedure, the facts as they emerge from district court opinions are more involved. In *U.S. v. Holmes County*[9] (Mississippi) two fire bombs were tossed into the home of a Negro couple who were housing four

---

[7]VI (1961) *RRLR* 1069.
[8]*U.S. v. Wood*, 295 F. 2d 772 (1961).
[9]IX (1964) *RRLR* 229.

registration workers including Robert Moses, then head of the Student Non-Violent Coordinating Committee, who was in town to lead a registration drive. Moses, his host, and three others were held for complicity of arson; Moses for impeding the sheriff's investigation of the fire. The county grand jury refused to indict on the arson charge. However, it was discovered that the Negro couple were not legally married so they were fined for unlawful cohabitation. Moses was fined $50 for impeding the investigation. The Attorney General sought an injunction against intimidation and misuse of the state's criminal processes. District Judge Cox ruled that the arrests were not improper and declined to grant any relief. He felt there could be no relation between the alleged arson and Moses' leadership in the voter registration campaign, since no local people of either race were interested in it.

Nor was the Government any more successful in a suit that sought to prevent alleged harassment of voter registration workers by officials of Dallas County, Alabama. Named as defendants were the county solicitor [prosecutor], Sheriff James Clark, Jr., several other county officials, and the Dallas County Citizens Council. The Government requested that they be enjoined from harassing voter registration efforts. The complaint stated that Sheriff Clarke and his officers attended voter registration meetings to record what was said and to take the names and auto license numbers of persons in attendance. There were also charges of baseless arrests of persons engaged in voter registration activities. In *United States v. Dallas County, et al.*[10] District Judge Thomas ruled that there was no element of intimidation in these proceedings. Attendance by the sheriff and his deputies at civil rights meetings was in line with their responsibility to maintain good order there. On one occasion the sheriff had rerouted a group of out-of-county cars away from the meeting, thus possibly averting disorder. One person had, indeed, been arrested while questioning persons waiting in the voter

[10]229 F. Supp. 1014 (1964).

registration line, but this was held to be failure to obey a lawful order. Another leader of the voter registration drive, Bernard Lafayete, had been charged with vagrancy. He was acquitted in his trial when it was shown that he was employed by the Student Non-Violent Coordinating Committee. However, Judge Thomas ruled that there was no harassment here. The arrest was based on "probable cause" since testimony from the sheriff's deputies and informers indicated that Lafayete had been seen begging. Nor was there any harassment involved in the arrest of another registration leader who was charged with driving with only one headlight and for giving a different name from that shown on his driver's license.

The Justice Department was a little more successful in another Mississippi case, U.S. v. City of Greenwood.[11] Eight registration workers were convicted after they and about 100 local Negroes walked to the city hall to protest the shooting into the home of a Negro registration worker. The eight workers were sentenced to four months and $200 fines each. The Government sought an injunction against the city and four of its officials to restrain them from interference with the registration drive. After more than a year of involved negotiations, the city agreed to set aside the convictions and to cease interference with registration activities, and the Attorney General agreed to dismiss the case.

The Attorney General likewise was able to do a little better in U.S. v. Mathews, et al.[12] Defendants were the sheriff of Terrell County, Georgia, two of his deputies, and several officials of the city of Sasser. The Government's suit called for an order restraining prosecution of two SNCC registration workers for vagrancy. Eventually there was worked out a consent decree enjoining the defendants from threatening, searching, arresting, or otherwise discouraging persons from

[11]New York Times, April 1-2, 1963. Congressional Quarterly, April 5, 1963, p. 527. U.S. Congress, Senate, Committee on the Judiciary, Hearings, Voting Rights, 89th Cong., 1st Session, 1965, pp. 1302-1303.
[12]IX (1964) RRLR 225.

registering and from refusing reasonable police protection to all persons in need thereof.

Yet Section (b) is hard to apply when the facts are more complex. *U.S. v. LeFlore County*[13] (Mississippi) began with the release of noxious fumes in a church where a registration drive was being held in a small town near Greenwood. Negroes tried unsuccessfully to contact Webber, a deputy sheriff. Then they decided to walk to Webber's home to appeal for protection in person. As they approached it, they were set upon by a small group of Negroes who threw bottles and bricks at them. Webber and another deputy sheriff promptly arrived and arrested 57 of those attacked. The next day they were convicted on charges of disturbing the peace by blocking public roads and throwing bottles and bricks. The men were sentenced to six months in jail and fines of $500; the women four months and $200. After a three-day hearing a district judge ruled that the Government had not established a violation of 1971(b).

U.S. v. Edwards, et al.[14] arose out of an incident in the Rankin County, Mississippi, Courthouse. Three Negroes entered the registrar's office. Two of them wanted to register; the third, Grim, was merely a spectator. It was a busy day in the registrar's office, and the office was small. Grim was in the way and was asked to move. He refused. Sheriff Edwards seized his blackjack, advanced upon Grim, and administered him a severe beating. Now the deputy sheriff rushed into the room and proceded to beat up the other two Negroes who were not—as the district court put it—"doing anything to provoke an assault."

The Government sued for an injunction against any further intimidation of prospective Negro voters by the sheriff. District Judge Cox, while holding this a deplorable attack, declined to issue an injunction. He reasoned that this was an

---

[13]Department of Justice news release dated June 28, 1963. Senate Committee on the Judiciary, 1965, pp. 1310-1311.

[14]IX (1964) *RRLR* 800.

isolated event, not part of a planned course of action. Since the event was unlikely to recur, no injunction was necessary. The Court of Appeals upheld Judge Cox by a two-to-one vote.[15] The majority found "no clear abuse of discretion" by the trial judge, nor were the findings of the trial court "clearly erroneous."

Justice Brown, the dissenter, declined to regard the beatings as isolated events but felt they should be viewed against Mississippi's "steelhard, inflexible, undeviating official policy of segregation." Noting that only 112 Negroes but 12,000 whites were registered in a county 37 per cent Negro, Judge Brown continued, "Where a sheriff and his deputy in the house of the law—the Courthouse—whip Negroes in the exercise of these fundamental rights, the effect is not hard to imagine. Nothing could be more discouraging than the fear that what happened to Grim, Davis, and Carr was the fate of others seeking this precious right."

A novel type of coercion is presented in *U.S. v. Warner*.[16] In May, 1960, during congressional debate on the Civil Rights Act of 1960, the Mississippi Legislature passed several statutes[17] which made it unlawful to make false statements to any representatives of any branch of the federal government and specifically any representative of the FBI or the Civil Rights Commission. The complaint stemmed from another voting suit in which Judge Cox ruled that the county registrar had discriminated against certain Negro applicants. However, he asked that the Justice Department look into possible perjury by two Negro witnesses, Andrew Kendrick, Jr., and William Goff. The Criminal Division of the Department of Justice investigated the matter and concluded that the facts did not establish a violation of federal law. Then the attorney who represented the registrar in the voting suit filed affidavits in a state court charging Kendrick and Goff with perjury. A

[15]333 F. 2d 575 (1964).
[16]IX (1964) *RRLR* 1101.
[17]Sec. 2155.4, 2155.5, and 2155.6 of the *Mississippi Code*.

grand jury indicted them, and Warner was the prosecuting attorney who would try the case. The Justice Department asserted that both the prosecution and the State's false-statements statutes were designed to intimidate illegally and discourage Negroes from seeking to vote.

In a brief opinion District Judge Mize ruled in favor of the Government. Quoting an 1890 U.S. Supreme Court case which held that one cannot be prosecuted in a state court for any sworn statements before a federal agency, the judge ordered the prosecution stopped, bail returned, and general non-interference with voting rights.

It must be borne in mind that the protection against intimidation or coercion contained in 1971 (b) applies only to instances where a specified defendant is named. And the person mandamused or enjoined must be the person engaged in the intimidation. The case of *Moses v. Kennedy*[18] clarifies this idea. The plaintiffs, Robert Moses and others, alleged that various Mississippi state and local officals were beating them up while they attempted to conduct registration drives. In their suit they asked that the Justice Department and the FBI be mandamused to protect them in their constitutional rights. District Judge Youngdahl of the District Court of the District of Columbia denied the plea. The decision held that it is the responsibility of the executive to see that all laws are faithfully enforced; courts cannot do this, nor has any aspect of recent civil rights legislation changed this usual rule. Moreover, the case was held to state no real controversy with a named federal official.

Section 1971(b) has some accomplishments to its credit, but in a larger sense its value has been limited. The Government bears a twofold burden. It must prove, first, the existence of intimidation, threats, or coercion, and second, that the intent of the intimidation, threat, or coercion was to interfere with the right to vote. The difficulty of demonstrating both these points is illustrated by the preceding cases, par-

[18]219 F. Supp. 762 (1963).

ticularly those in the area of what the Justice Department calls "baseless arrests." If a registration worker is driving with only one headlight and with an expired driver's license, it is hard to argue that the arrest is clearly baseless. Moreover, even when the Government won a suit to restrain coercion, the victory did not usually enfranchise anyone. Local officials were still free to retire to their second line of defense—the registration office—where they held the line against Negro registration through the use of what might be generally called "double standards."

DISCRIMINATION

The Struggle for the Records

Only a minority of the total number of suits have arisen under a claim of coercion or intimidation. The greater number of suits have involved section 1971(a) which prohibits racial discrimination in voting. The section reads:

> All citizens of the United States who are otherwise qualified by law to vote at any election . . . shall be entitled to vote at all such elections without distinction of race, color, . . .; any constitution, law, custom, usage, or regulation of any state . . . to the contrary notwithstanding.

In many areas of the Deep South it is common knowledge that Negroes were prevented from voting or certainly discouraged from registering and voting. However, this "common knowledge" is not enough to persuade a federal judge. The first step in proving discrimination is to secure a county's registration records. Without the records one cannot demonstrate even so basic a fact as that 98 per cent of whites of voting age in the county are registered whereas the corresponding figure for Negroes is 2 per cent. The demonstration of this disproportion is not necessarily persuasive; it might be coincidental. In addition, the records may often be used to demonstrate that the registration imbalance is due to the rigorous standards required of Negroes and the very indulgent standards applied to whites. Both federal and state officials are aware of the importance of access to the records. It will be recalled that the 1960 act requires that all election and registration records be preserved, in effect, indefinitely, and that any record or paper thus preserved must be made available by the person having custody of it for inspection or reproduction by a representative of the Attorney General. Earthy incidents recounted in cases attest to the importance that registrars attach to these records. In *U.S. v. Cartwright*[19] two members of the Elmore County, Alabama, Board of Registrars, learning of a forthcoming FBI investigation of their records, quietly carried a large supply of records to the city dump and set them on fire. Both Alabama and Mississippi legislatures passed laws permitting (not requiring) registrars to dispose of these records. While these state laws are in conflict with the federal law and therefore unconstitutional, their passage indicates the general agreement on the importance of access to records.

One may reasonably infer that a person who has nothing to conceal will voluntarily permit inspection of his records. Contrariwise, tenacious litigation to prevent inspection of the records suggests that a registrar has something to hide. By January, 1964, the Justice Department had asked to inspect the records of 100 counties. In 38 instances, court action had to be brought to secure access.[20] It is a tribute to the ingenuity of defense attorneys that the Department should have to resort to the courts in 38 instances. It would seem that the third section of Title III of 1960 Civil Rights Act is plain enough. It provides:

> Any record or paper required by section 301 to be retained and preserved shall, upon demand in writing by the Attorney

[19]230 F. Supp. 873 (1964).
[20]U.S. Congress, House, Subcommittee of the Committee on Appropriations, *Hearings, Departments of State, Justice, and Commerce,* 88th Cong., 2nd Session, 1964, p. 136.

> General or his representative directed to the person having
> custody, possession, or control of such record or paper, be
> made available for inspection, reproduction, and copying
> at the principal office of such custodian by the Attorney
> General or his representative. This demand shall contain
> a statement of the basis or purpose therefor.

Yet great ingenuity may be exercised here. The question may
be raised over who has actual physical custody of the records
at a given time since the Government must address its demand
to "the person having custody . . ." What happens if the
registrar has temporarily given custody of the records to the
county solicitor or the county grand jury? In *U.S. v. Majors*[21]
the Attorney General made a formal request on April 13,
1961, that the records be made available for photographing.
Upon refusal, the case was taken to court, and a trial held
on October 30, 1961. The defendant held that the records
were in the hands of the grand jury and not in the custody of
the board of registrars. On February 19, 1962, the district
court finally ruled in favor of the Government, holding that
all records were in daily use by the defendant. This technicality
delayed the Attorney General nearly a year. A monumentally
absurd legal issue arises when a voting registrar holds
another job and title. In the case of *Kennedy v. Owen*[22]
the Government had asked the district judge for an inspection
order directing the circuit clerks of seven Mississippi counties
to make their records available for inspection. Under Mississippi law a registrar is also the circuit clerk. U.S. District
Judge Cox granted an inspection order as to the records
each defendant possessed in his capacity as circuit clerk but
not as registrar. The Court of Appeals would have none of
this quibble and ruled that the records be made available.

The most fertile source of delaying action was the defense
effort to construe this section as a criminal prosecution in
which the defendant could not have his papers searched

[21]VII (1962) *RRLR* 463.
[22]321 F. 2d 116 (1963).

unless there were a precise description of the records that were wanted. This reading of the act also raised the question whether a registrar must make available the records of his predecessor. It was necessary to try a series of cases to clarify the meaning of Title III. The struggle to inspect the records of Wilcox County, Alabama, took two years. Eventually several cases stated with considerable clarity the meaning of this part of the law—namely Title III. In *Kennedy v. Lynd*[23] the circuit court was at pains to emphasize that there was here no question of the relevancy of the documents, that is, the Government need not demonstrate that a document is relevant to the case before examining it. Nor is there any question of time limit; establishing a pattern or practice of discrimination may require a study of documents that goes back many years. In other respects, Title III is unlike a traditional criminal action. Title III requires that "every officer of election shall retain and preserve . . . all records and papers which come into his possession relating to any application, registration . . ." Congress has specified what papers must be preserved. Hence, there can be no room for a quibble about what papers are to be made available to the Attorney General. The law governing preservation and examining of papers applies to *all* papers, not merely those that some applicant thinks would demonstrate discrimination against him. Nor does it make any difference whether there has been a change of registrars. Records of earlier registrars cannot be denied on the theory that an office-holder cannot be held accountable for the acts of his predecessor. The registrar is not accused of having violated constitutional rights. He is a party to the suit because he has custody of records. The Court of Appeals emphasized that there was no hidden meaning in the final sentence of Title III which states that the Attorney General's demand "contain a statement of the

---

[23]306 F. 2d 222 (1962). This case was consolidated with *Kennedy v. Bryce* and three other cases.

basis and purpose thereof." In another case[24] when counsel representing a Mississippi registrar attempted to read much into this statement, the court went into the legislative history of the act. It quoted Senator Keating as stating to his colleagues, "Clearly a sufficient statement would be assertion that the demand was made for the purpose of investigating possible violations of a federal statute." No showing even of a *prima facie* case of violation of federal law need be made. Mississippi continued to fight on this issue by taking the case to the Supreme Court where certiorari was denied.[25]

Securing the records is the first step in a laborious process, which may or may not justify the filing of a suit which may or may not result in a court order enfranchising some Negroes. From the standpoint of the determined enemy of Negro voting, all litigation on the get-the-records issue has been a strategy of defense-in-depth. You fight at the outposts to stave off the day when you will have to defend the inner citadel. Yet the Justice Department has had to spend a great part of its energies trying to lay hands on the raw materials out of which a case may possibly be made. While the Government has eventually won all these get-the-records cases, the defense tactics have compelled tedious litigation over technicalities and postponed consideration by the courts of substantive issues, thereby lessening the effectiveness of civil rights legislation.

Purges

Delaying tactics eventually lose. Registrars must eventually permit examination of their records, and the Justice Department searches them for evidence of discrimination. Discrimination may occur at any stage of the process of registration and voting, and Congress recognized this and sought to

[24]*Coleman v. Kennedy,* 313 F. 2d 867 (1963).
[25]373 U.S. 950 (1963).

give inclusive protection by the broad definition given the word "vote" in Title VI of the Civil Rights Act of 1960.

> When used in this subsection the word "vote" includes all action necessary to make a vote effective including, but not limited to, registration or any other action required by State law prerequisite to voting, casting a ballot, and having such ballot counted and included in the appropriate totals of votes cast . . .

The voter purge is a form of discrimination based on a peculiarity of the Louisiana election law. Purge cases are confined to that state. The law permits any registered voter to challenge the legality of the registration of any other registered voter. The Citizens Council of the state discovered this ancient provision on the statute books. Working oftentimes in cooperation with parish registrars, they examined the registration forms of Negro voters in order to find errors in spelling, blank spaces where information should have been supplied, or other technicalities that would support the claim that the original registration had been fraudulent. In the case of *U.S. v. McElveen* [26] (involving the purging from the registration book of Washington Parish of 1,377 Negro voters—98 per cent of all Negro registrants—and of only 10 white voters for alleged deficiencies in their application forms) the Government was able to demonstrate that at least 50 per cent of the unchallenged applications of white voters had the same defects. The court ordered the purged Negroes restored to the registration rolls. A similar case was *U.S. v. Association of Citizens Councils of Louisiana*,[27] involving a purge in Bienville Parish. Here the district court ordered the restoration of 570 Negroes to the registration rolls and enjoined the registrar from administering the laws in a racially discriminatory fashion in the future. *U.S. v. Wilder*[28] involved a purge, plus other discriminatory practices. The registrar, Mrs. Wilder,

[26] 180 F. Supp. 10 (1960).
[27] 196 F. Supp. 908 (1961).
[28] 222 F. Supp. 749 (1963).

and the local Citizens Council challenged the status of 953 of the 1,122 Negro voters and 13 of the more than 5,000 whites. Notices of purge were mailed out the day the registration books were closed in preparation for the November, 1956, general election. Immediately thereafter Jackson Parish adopted a permanent registration system so that all persons registered on January 1, 1957, were automatically given permanent registration status. Thereafter, standards were raised so that application cards had to be filled out perfectly. This raising of standards affected practically all Negroes, but only those whites not yet of voting age. The Attorney General was able to demonstrate that the challenges were based on errors and omissions made by 75 per cent of the white voters also, and the district court decreed, among other things, that the 953 purged names be restored to the voting list.

Purge cases are less difficult for the Government than some other types. Once the registration records have been made available, it is difficult for a judge to reach any conclusion other than that gross discrimination has taken place. This is not to suggest that the handling of the purge cases is always swift or simple. In *U.S. v. Wilder* the purge occurred in October, 1956; the decision ordering the names restored was rendered in 1963. The purge cases rectify past injustices, but they made no net increase in the number of Negro voters. They recapture ground lost to an earlier segregationist attack, but no additional county is brought under the Fifteenth Amendment. No hitherto unregistered Negro is registered by this type of case.

The several other forms of discrimination will be treated in approximately the chronological order that they would take place in the registration process. On a few occasions Negroes have difficulty finding the registration officals. There is a touch of hide-and-seek here. During much of the period 1946 to 1961 Macon County, Alabama, had no functioning board of registrars. In Bullock County, Alabama, Negroes were told that there would be no registration on July 4, yet the board worked and received applications from whites on that date.[29] In *U.S. v. Duke*,[30] involving Panola County, Mississippi, Negro applicants were told that the registrar could not find the questionnaire forms. Moreover, there were two courthouses in the county, which gave opportunity for sending voters back and forth between the two courthouses. It was necessary to take this case to the Court of Appeals before these two practices were regarded as discriminatory.

Slowdown

Courts are willing to find discrimination in instances where white applicants are given prompt service whereas would-be Negro registrants are subjected to lengthy delays, a practice popularly known as the "slowdown." In the Bullock County case the decision noted that the board of registrars received an average of only 24 applications on each registration day. However, on one day when all applicants were white, the board received 45 applications. Negroes appearing at the board's office were asked to sign a priority list. Some 700 Negroes signed the list, yet in the course of five months, with the board meeting twice a month, only 250 of these had an opportunity to attempt to register. Likewise, Negroes were required to go into a small room in groups of eight to fill out the form, and each group of eight was required to wait until its slowest member had finished. Needless to say, whites were not subjected to this platoon system. Judicial notice of a similar situation was taken in *U.S. v. Clement*.[31] Here Negroes had to go into the registrar's office one at the time, and no other applicant could enter until his predecessor had left, yet as many as four whites were allowed in the registrar's office at the same time. *U.S. v. Duke*[32] noted that Negro

[29]*U.S. v. Alabama, et al.*, VII (1962) *RRLR* 1146.
[30]332 F. 2d 759 (1964).
[31]231 F. Supp. 913 (1964).
[32]332 F. 2d 759 (1964).

applicants had to wait 25 or 30 minutes before they were given any attention or service.

The Government usually won suits alleging a slowdown, at least on appeal, yet it lost one case having all the earmarks of an ingenious type of slowdown. This was the Hinds County, Mississippi, case of *U.S. v. Ashford.*[33] The Justice Department alleged the following facts: first, only 500 of the 7,000 registered voters on the registration rolls were Negro. Second, there was a Negro registration drive in progress, aimed at getting more colored voters involved in the 1963 gubernatorial primary. The Justice Department claimed that between June 12 and July 5, some 700 Negroes tried to register but found facilities lacking. On July 3, Registrar Ashford went to a state court, claiming that his office was swamped, and asked for and received a court order closing the registration books. The Justice Department claimed that neither it nor the county's citizens were given an opportunity to be heard at the state court hearing. Further, the Government's suit for reopening the books alleged that at the time the 700 Negroes unsuccessfully attempted to register, 129 whites applied and 124 were accepted. It also noted that in the past the registrar's office had been capable of processing over 100 applications a day. In any event, District Judge Cox held the "closing of the books non-discriminatory." He did rule that if and when the registration books were opened, the applicants must be treated on a first-come, first-served basis.

An odd procedure that the courts have generally been willing to recognize as discriminatory is the requirement of the voucher, or identifier. The registration laws of Alabama and Louisiana permit a registrar to require an applicant to secure a registered voter to swear that the applicant is the person he claims to be and has actually met the state and county residence requirements. The laws of most states guard against the danger of impersonation or inadequate residence by having the applicant swear to this, with a per-

[33]*New York Times,* July 14, 1963, p. 48.

jury prosecution being the sanction. This practice was involved in the Bullock County case.[34] At the time of the trial
in March, 1961, the county had only six registered Negroes.
The board had exercised a touch of ingenuity by ruling that no
registered voter could vouch for more than one applicant
per year. The board justified its action by reference to the
Alabama law which empowers registrars to make minor rulings
designed to expedite business. In the segregationist climate
of the county no white person was willing to vouch for a
Negro. A teacher of arithmetic might seize on this situation
for an examination question: at this rate of registration and
vouching, in what year will there be 500 colored registrants?
The court enjoined the annual-limit practice.

Two Louisiana cases also involved an identifier requirement.
Both cases were decided in favor of the Government. *U.S.
v. Ward*[35] arose in Madison Parish, where no Negro had been
registered during this century. Defendant registrar, Miss
Ward, did not require identifiers for white applicants she
knew; she required identifiers for all Negro applicants. She
testified she knew most of the whites and very few of the
Negroes. On August 28, 1961, four Negroes appeared at her
office to try to register. They were required to get two voters
to identify them. The mayor of the city of Tallulah declined
to act as identifier, and no lesser citizen would help. District
Judge Dawkins ruled that the identifier requirement was a
discriminatory practice. He decreed that hereafter Miss Ward
accept as proof of identity such legal documentary proof as
drivers licenses, selective service cards, library cards, etc.
In *U.S. v. Manning*,[36] involving East Carroll Parish, no white
voter would identify a Negro although no white voters had
any trouble with the identification requirement. Here, too,
the registrar was ordered to accept reasonable documentary
proof of identity. Rather than obey the order, the registrar

---

[34]*U.S. v. Alabama et al.*, VII (1962) *RRLR* 1146.
[35]222 F. Supp. 617 (1963).
[36]205 F. Supp. 172 (1962).

resigned. Subsequent litigation was necessary before the enforcement of the judge's order that 26 out of 78 Negro applicants be registered.

In *U.S. v. Hines*,[37] involving Sumter County, Alabama, the district judge listed under his findings of discrimination the requirement of a voucher, who usually had to be white, and the assistance given to whites, but not Negroes, in locating a voucher.

The use of a voucher or a supporting witness may seem so obvious a technique of discrimination that any judge would promptly rule in favor of the Government. This view underestimates the frustrations and problems of the Justice Department. Consider the case of *U.S. v. Logue*,[38] involving Wilcox County, Alabama. Not a single Negro was registered in this 70-per-cent-Negro county. In 1963, 29 Negroes applied; all were rejected for failure to have a registered voter to vouch for them. The Government asked the court to set aside the voucher requirement as clearly discriminatory. The court refused. The judge declined to see any precedent in either the *Manning* or the *Ward* cases because in those cases there was an "intent" to discriminate. In Wilcox County, everyone —black or white—was required to secure a voucher; hence, the board had discriminated against no one. The Court of Appeals reversed the decision,[39] but some 13 months elapsed between the decision of the district court and that of the Court of Appeals.

The Double Standard

Courts are usually willing to take notice of and enjoin as discriminatory the practice of registrars assisting whites, but not Negroes, in the filling out of application forms. The states of Louisiana, Mississippi, and Alabama required a would-be voter to fill out an application form of some length

---

[37]IX (1964) *RRLR* 1333.
[38]IX (1964) *RRLR* 770.
[39]344 F. 2d 290 (1965).

and difficulty. For example, the Alabama form contained 21 questions, was two printed pages in length, and had the degree of reading difficulty and word knowledge expected of a person with at least an eighth-grade education. Southern folklore assumes that when a white person reaches his twenty-first birthday he has a "right" to vote. This is an attribute of citizenship acquired simply by reaching one's majority. Hence, semi-literate whites must not be burdened with these forms. The law requires that the forms be filled out in one's own handwriting and without assistance, but, as applied to whites, it is notable more in the breach than in the observance. Yet the law is often applied strictly to Negroes. In several cases judges were willing to take judicial notice of this practice and to enjoin its continuance. In *U.S. v. Penton*[40] (Montgomery County, Alabama) the judge noted that the board filled out for whites, but not for Negroes, the question which requires the applicant to state the date at which he became a *bona fide* resident of the state, county, and precinct. Judicial notice of the practice of assisting whites in filling out their forms without corresponding assistance for Negroes was mentioned in the judge's findings of discrimination in the following cases: *U.S. v. Hines*,[41] *U.S. v. Wilder*,[42] and *U.S. v. Ford*.[43] In the Macon County case the judge included assistance to semi-literate whites as one of the several forms of discrimination.

Presumably the most complete form of assistance to be given whites—carrying the whole matter to its logical conclusion—is not requiring whites to fill out application forms at all. In the long and amazing case of *U.S. v. Lynd*[44] the Circuit Court ruled that among the facts established by the Government was the fact that prior to January 31, 1961, most of the white applicants were permitted to register with-

[40]212 F. Supp. 193 (1962).
[41]IX (1964) *RRLR* 1333.
[42]222 F. Supp. 749 (1963).
[43]IX (1964) *RRLR* 1331.
[44]301 F. 2d 818 (1962).

out even filling out an application form. In *U.S. v. Ramsey*,[45] illiterate whites were found to have been commonly registered, some whites without even appearing at the registrar's office. When the case reached the Court of Appeals,[46] a dissenting judge was more specific and noted that 1,500 whites were registered without ever having set foot in the registrar's office.

Giving more difficult tests to Negroes than to whites has been adjudged discriminatory. Southern folklore abounds with stories of such tests. The prototype involves the efforts of a Negro professor to become registered. He had no trouble reading the Constitution in English, nor in French or German, since he taught both of these languages. Finally he is asked to translate a section of the Constitution printed in Chinese. Most versions have the Negro educator stating sadly, "This is Chinese and it says that no Negro can vote in this county." Thigh-slapping and guffaws follow.

In practice this level of crudity has not been reached, but approximations of it have appeared. In the Macon County, Alabama, case[47] the court noted that Negroes were always required to demonstrate a reading knowledge of the U.S. Constitution, usually Article II. The few whites who were subjected to any reading test were required to read a much shorter passage. A passage in the Louisiana Constitution requires that applicants not only read the Constitution but understand and explain the Constitution—obviously to the satisfaction of a registrar who is not a constitutional lawyer. In *U.S. v. Wilder*[48] a district judge enjoined the use of this constitutional interpretation test by the registrar of Jackson Parish. Its use resulted in the rejection of 23 Negro school teachers, although the registrar approved white applicants who were unable to read the application form. A similar

[45]VIII (1963) *RRLR* 156.
[46]331 F. 2d 824 (1964).
[47]*U.S. v. Alabama*, 192 F. Supp. 677 (1961).
[48]222 F. Supp. 749 (1963).

finding of discrimination was made in *U.S. v. Clement*,[49] in which it was found that the registrar of Webster Parish required an oral interpretation test of Negroes only. In *U.S. v. Atkins*[50] a similar finding was made only after appeal to the Circuit Court. This court enjoined oral questions unless the board kept records of the exact questions asked and the answers given by each applicant.

A weakness of this form of discrimination is that it is too obvious. A subtler method is to have applicants of both races complete the same application form but then judge the efforts of colored applicants rigorously and those of white applicants indulgently. The tactics in Louisiana, Mississippi, and Alabama have been to go over the application forms of Negroes with a fine-tooth comb in order to find what the courts have come to call "technical and inconsequential" errors. This type of discrimination emphasizes again the importance to the Government of securing the application forms for photostating and examination. Without the forms for all applicants—white and colored—one cannot demonstrate discrimination. A landmark case in this area is *U.S. v. George Penton*.[51] The district judge observed:

> Prior to June 1, 1960 the Board registered only 54 Negro applicants who had technical errors appearing in their questionnaires; up until the same time the Board rejected only 74 whites for the same type of errors. The rejection of whites subsequent to June, 1960 (and particularly since 1961, when it became apparent that this case was to be filed) impresses this Court as being nothing more than a sham and an attempt on the part of the Board to disguise their past discriminatory practices. Rejection of these white applicants approaches the ridiculous . . .
>
> The Court has made a careful study and analysis of both the white accepted and the Negro rejected applicants. 1,070 white applicants whose application contained errors were accepted in this five-year period . . .

[49] 231 F. Supp. 913 (1964).
[50] 323 F. 2d 733 (1963), Dallas County, Alabama.
[51] 212 F. Supp. 193 (1962), Montgomery County, Alabama.

In five other Alabama cases[52] this version of the double standard was ruled discriminatory and enjoined. Likewise in three Louisiana cases[53] the district court enjoined these double standards.

Only occasionally is a district court not persuaded by double standards. The court's observation in *U.S. v. Atkins*[54] is untypical: ". . . there may be differences of opinion on many of these applications. There is a human element involved in the grading of any examination paper." This decision was eventually overruled by the Court of Appeals.[55] In Mississippi in the fantastic case of *U.S. v. Lynd* the trial judge saw no double standards, but in the Court of Appeals the justices ruled that the Government had established the existence of double standards. Item: five Hattiesburg school teachers (Negro), three of them with M.A. degrees, were rejected, although defendants were unable to name a single white person they had rejected.[56] However, on the illegality of double standards, the courts have been in general agreement, so much so, in fact, that it would seem that their consensus has been embodied in Title I, Section 101 (b) of the Civil Rights Act of 1964, which makes it illegal for any person acting under color of law to

> deny the right of any individual to vote in any Federal Election because of an error or omission on any record or paper relating to any application, registration, or other act requisite to voting, if such error or omission is not material in determining whether such individual is qualified under State law to vote in such election.

[52]*U.S. v. Alabama*, 192 F. Supp. 677 (1961), Macon County.
   U.S. v. Mayton, VII (1962) *RRLR* 1136, Perry County.
   U.S. v. Ford, IX (1964) *RRLR* 1331, Choctaw County.
   U.S. v. Cartwright, 230 F. Supp. 873 (1964), Elmore County.
   U.S. v. Hines, IX (1964) *RRLR* 1333, Sumter County.
[53]*U.S. v. Wilder*, 222 F. Supp. 749 (1963), Jackson Parish.
   U.S. v. Clement, 231 F. Supp. 913 (1964), Webster Parish.
   U.S. v. Crawford, 229 F. Supp. 898 (1964), Red River Parish.
[54]210 F. Supp. 441 (1962).
[55]323 F. 2d 733 (1963).
[56]301 F. 2d 818 (1962).

Courts commonly find discriminatory the practice of failing to notify Negro applicants whether or not their applications have been approved. Negro applicants are permitted to fill out application forms without harassment. Then the application form is handed to the registrar, and that is the last that is heard of it. Courts have made findings of fact that boards have failed to notify Negro applicants whether or not their applications have been approved, and they have banned them as discriminatory in several Alabama cases.[57] In *U.S. v. George Penton*[58] the court noted that during the entire five-year period during which it found that discrimination occurred, the board failed to notify any of the rejected applicants that they had been rejected.

Another variant is to tell a rejected applicant that he failed but refuse to tell him why he failed. This prevents the rejectee from avoiding the same mistake a second time and probably makes more difficult the securing of legal redress. If one is kept in the dark about why he was rejected, he will have no grounds for arguing the impropriety of the rejection. This practice was noted and enjoined in the *Mayton* and *Ford* cases noted above as well as in *U.S. v. Cartwright*,[59] *U.S. v. Clement*,[60] and *U.S. v. Crawford*.[61]

A hybrid between assistance-for-whites-only and rejection for inconsequential omissions is rejection for failure to sign the proper number of oaths on the Alabama registration form. The Alabama form covers four printed pages. The last two pages are usually filled out by the board of registrars. However, on the first two pages there are three spaces in which the applicant must sign his name. At the outset the applicant is confronted with a first line reading, "I_____

[57]*U.S. v. Ford*, IX (1964) *RRLR* 1331.
   U.S. v. Hines, IX (1964) *RRLR* 1333.
   U.S. v. Alabama, 192 F. Supp. 677 (1961).
   U.S. v. Mayton, VII (1962) *RRLR* 1136.
[58]212 F. Supp. 193 (1962).
[59]230 F. Supp. 873 (1964).
[60]231 F. Supp. 913 (1964).
[61]229 F. Supp. 898 (1964).

do hereby apply . . . to register." Applicant must fill in his name in the blank space, then sign on another line to the effect that he does "herewith submit answers to the inter-rogatories propounded to me . . ." Finally, on the third page there is an oath that the applicant must sign, pledging his willingness to defend the Constitution and disavowing belief in the overthrow of government by unlawful means. It was the practice in several Alabama counties for registrars to call to the attention of each white applicant the need to sign his name in all three places. Negroes did not have this matter called to their attention, and they were therefore denied registration for failure to fill out their forms properly. This practice was held discriminatory in *U.S. v. Cartwright*,[62] and in *U.S. v. Penton*[63] Judge Johnson used rather forthright language in ruling this practice discriminatory.

Section 180 of the Alabama Constitution restricts the elect-orate to persons of "good character." Little evidence of dis-criminatory use of this clause appears except that in the decrees of two Alabama cases[64] boards are forbidden to dis-franchise on this ground unless the applicant has been given notice and hearing and has had revealed to him the nature of his bad character.

Double standards may also take the form of telling rejected Negro applicants that they may not reapply for six months. The Court of Appeals in the *Lynd*[65] case observed that the Government had established the fact that rejected Negroes were required to wait six months before reapplying although there was no statutory authorization for this. In *U.S. v. Atkins*[66] a district judge who ruled against the Government in its effort to establish half a dozen other forms of discrimina-tion was willing to enjoin the practice of forbidding rejected

[62]230 F. Supp. 873 (1964).
[63]212 F. Supp. 193 (1962).
[64]*U.S. v. Ford,* IX (1964) *RRLR* 1331.
    U.S. v. Atkins, 323 F. 2d 733 (1963).
[65]301 F. 2d 818 (1962).
[66]210 F. Supp. 441 (1962).

applicants from applying again for registration. He suggested that a 60-day waiting period between registration efforts would be reasonable. Similarly in *U.S. v. Mayton*[67] the same judge enjoined the Perry County (Alabama) board from refusing to permit rejected applicants to reapply as often as they wished after a 60-day waiting period after each rejection. Rejected whites encountered no barriers to reapplying whenever they chose.

Although logical exposition has required separate treatment of each of the above forms of discrimination, these forms do not appear separately in practice. Registrars bent on discrimination employ the whole arsenal of discriminatory techniques. Thus, court orders commonly list half a dozen practices that must not be employed in the future.

The Relevance of Statistics

A reasonable man may tire at this lengthy enumeration of forms of discrimination and ask impatiently, "Can't you prove discrimination with statistics?" Indeed, it might seem so. It was common knowledge for years that there was not a single registered Negro in either Lowndes or Wilcox counties in Alabama, and many such "zero" counties existed in Mississippi. Does this not in and of itself prove discrimination? No, not necessarily. In several cases the Government was unable to cite specific acts of discrimination to the satisfaction of district judges, not all of whom—it will be argued later—abhor discrimination. If no Negro has attempted to register for 50 years, has any Negro been discriminated against? What action shall a judge enjoin? Consider the difficulties of the Justice Department in *U.S. v. Duke*,[68] in which a district judge was not impressed by the statistical fact that the only Negro registered when the suit was filed was a man 92 years old who had registered in 1892. What did impress the judge was the small number of Negroes who had made an effort

[67]VII (1962) *RRLR* 1136.
[68]IX (1964) *RRLR* 788.

to register in recent years. Nor did statistics impress the
district judge in *U.S. v. Logue,*[69] where the Government sought
an injunction on the voucher requirement since none of
the 29 Negroes who made applications in 1963 was able to
get a registered voter to vouch for him. The court accepted
as established the fact that no Negroes were registered in
this 70-per-cent-Negro county but did not see in the total
situation a pattern or practice of discrimination. The court
refused to enjoin the voucher requirement since there was
no harassment or intimidation of these 29 applicants. Or a
court may agree that a mountain of statistics demonstrates
conclusively that registrars in earlier years have discriminated
flagrantly, yet hold that the more recently appointed board,
presently incumbent, is performing commendably and is
"unlikely to resume" the earlier statistically demonstrated discrimination.[70] Hence, no judicial relief is necessary.

With the passage of time, judges became more receptive
to statistics as a proof of discrimination. All three decisions
cited above were reversed by the Court of Appeals. The
use of statistics began with Alabama's Macon County case,
U.S. v. Alabama.[71] After the Government won its suit, the
State of Alabama appealed. The Court of Appeals[72] upheld
the district court: "After a trial comprising over 900 pages
of testimony from 53 witnesses, plus two huge boxes of documentary exhibits . . ." Later in its ruling the Court observed,
"In the problem of racial discrimination, statistics often tell
much, and Courts listen." This was the case that made
statistics respectable.

The willingness to look realistically at statistics was again
manifested by District Judge Frank Johnson in the Montgomery County case.[73] The decision noted that between
January 1, 1956, and January 1, 1961, the defendants reg-

[69]IX (1964) *RRLR* 770.
[70]*U.S. v. Atkins,* 210 F. Supp. 441 (1962).
[71]192 F. Supp. 677 (1961).
[72]*State of Alabama v. U.S.,* 304 F. 2d 583 (1962).
[73]*U.S. v. Penton,* 212 F. Supp. 193 (1962).

istered 96 per cent of white applicants but rejected 75 per cent of Negro applicants, including 710 who had more than 12 years of formal schooling. This group included 106 Negro school teachers. These observations were the first of a series of findings of fact that led to a ruling that discrimination had existed.

Two months later the Court of Appeals in *U.S. v. Dogan*[74] set aside the district court's refusal to grant an injunction, holding that the district judge was clearly in error in failing to do so. They quoted approvingly the language of *Alabama v. U.S.*, "In the problem of racial discrimination, statistics often tell much, and Courts listen." The Court then continued with a recital of the classic situation of nearly all the adult whites in the county being registered and no Negroes even being permitted to pay their poll tax. In the same year a decision was rendered in *U.S. v. Wilder*,[75] in which the Court observed that between October, 1956, and September, 1962, defendant Registrar Wilder rejected 64 per cent of Negro applicants and only about two per cent of white applicants. By April, 1964, in Alabama, United States District Judge Thomas was citing registration figures in ruling in favor of the Government in the Choctaw County case, *U.S. v. Ford*.[76] The decision noted that in February, 1963, there were 3,697 white registrants and 176 Negroes. Of the Negroes, 137 had been registered prior to November, 1959. Between the latter date and the trial in February, 1963, the defendants had registered 782 whites and rejected two; in the same period they had registered 40 Negroes and rejected 260.

Clearly, with the passage of time the willingness to consider registration statistics as part of the evidence has increased. Consider the well-worded statement of District

---

[74] 314 F. 2d 767 (1963).
[75] 222 F. Supp. 749 (1963).
[76] IX (1964) *RRLR* 1331.

Judge Grooms when in September, 1964, he ruled in favor of the Government in the Sumter County case:[77]

> With a Negro population in Sumter County of more than twice that of the white, and with a registration of 3,238 whites and 315 Negroes and with a rejection of 47.2 per cent of Negro applications since May, 1964, as compared with 1.7 per cent of white applications, there is created a presumption that Negro citizens have been deprived, and are being deprived, of the right to register or vote because of race or color. The evidence offered by the defendants has not overcome this presumption.

Note the last sentence and particularly the word *presumption*. The judge is saying, in effect, that it looks odd when half of the Negro applicants are rejected but practically none of the white applicants and the burden is on the defendants to explain away this peculiarity.

Pattern or Practice

After the presentation of evidence concerning discrimination, the Attorney General is empowered under the Civil Rights Act of 1960 to request a district court to find a "pattern or practice" of discrimination. The discrimination, thus, is not against an isolated individual. The Attorney General must first persuade the court that some one person has been discriminated against. However, the request for a finding of pattern or practice may be contained in the same action.[78] From the Government's standpoint, securing a ruling of a pattern or practice is advantageous, although not a cure-all. If a judge sees no pattern of discrimination, he will have no logical reason for granting any vigorous or far-reaching relief. *U.S. v. Mississippi and Wood*[79] illustrates the relationship between not finding a pattern or practice and the issuance

[77]*U.S. v. Hines,* IX (1964) *RRLR* 1333.
[78]*U.S. v. Dogan,* 314 F. 2d 767 (1963).
[79]VIII (1963) *RRLR* 1537.

of a very modest decree. The district judge ruled, "There is
no need . . . for any finding . . . as to pattern or practice.
There were relatively so few Negroes who applied to register
to vote that it would be difficult if not impossible to make
a fair determination on that question . . ." However, Judge
Cox felt that Registrar Wood had discriminated against the
few Negroes who had applied. The decree ordered him to
register within five days one particular Negro, Masie Bullock.
The four parts of his order amounted to instructing the registrar to register no more illiterates of either race. When the
Court of Appeals overruled Judge Cox,[80] they made an in-
teresting clarification of the law. They ruled that Judge
Cox's recitation of certain discriminatory acts was tantamount
to finding a pattern or practice. Not only had the trial court
erred in not finding a pattern, but the very recitation of discriminatory acts by the trial court was essentially establishing
the existence of the pattern which this Court declined to
find. "No magic phrase need be said to set in train the
remedy provided in number 1971 (e)." A trial judge may
be told that his finding of the nonexistence of a pattern or
practice is a clearly erroneous finding, and he may be overruled. The same legal point about a trial judge not having
to utter a "magic phrase" appears in *U.S. v. Ramsey*.[81] Here
a district judge found that eight Negroes were indeed discriminated against but ruled that this was the result of the
loose and inefficient manner in which the 82-year-old registrar ran his office. Since no intentional pattern of discrimination existed, the judge found it unnecessary to rule one way
or another on the existence of a pattern or practice. On
appeal,[82] the Court ruled that the trial judge had, in fact,
ruled that no pattern existed and that his decision on this
point was clearly erroneous. This idea that the district judge
actually found a pattern or practice even though he did not

[80]339 F. 2d 679 (1964).
[81]VIII (1963) *RRLR* 156.
[82]*U.S., Appellant v. Ramsey*, 331 F. 2d 824 (1964).

enunciate those precise words appeared in *U.S. v. Hon. Dan H. Thomas.*[83] In ruling on an appeal of Judge Thomas's decision in *U.S. v. Mayton* the Court of Appeals noticed that the judge had in the course of his decision indicated that "defendants have engaged in acts . . . which have had the purpose and effect of depriving Negroes of their right to register without distinction of race or color."

When a judge couples a finding of a pattern or practice with a vigorous decree, as in the *Penton* case, the results may be impressive. After describing in considerable detail the evidence of discrimination practiced by the Montgomery County registrars, the court stated that when a pattern or practice of discrimination is demonstrated—such as was shown here—the rejected Negro applicants may apply to a federal court to be registered. The court must then determine the standards that have actually been applied to white applicants throughout the period of discrimination. Once the "actual requirements" had been defined, the judge ordered immediate registration of some 1,100 Negroes who had met these "actual requirements." Note the one-step character of this decision. In one and the same case the Government asked for a pattern-or-practice finding and, once it was granted, enabled the rejected Negro applicants to apply to the court for immediate registration.

Less dramatic findings of pattern or practice appeared in the *Crawford*[84] and *Clement*[85] cases. In *U.S. v. Hines*[86] District Judge Grooms summarized his findings of discrimination with the statement that "Such deprivations have been and are pursuant to a pattern or practice of racial discrimination."

[83]335 F. 2d 153 (1964).
[84]229 F. Supp. 898 (1964).
[85]231 F. Supp. 913 (1964).
[86]IX (1964) *RRLR* 1333.

Does Raising the Standards Constitute Discrimination?

Most Deep South states have been indulgent about the requirements exacted of whites wishing to register. At a period of history when large numbers of Negroes suddenly want to register, is it discriminatory for a state to raise its standards of literacy? In the abstract, there is no doubt that a state can raise its standards, but can it in this historical context? The problem is well illustrated by Alabama's Dallas County case.[87] Some time around January, 1961, Dallas County secured the services of a new board of registrars, which applied more exacting standards to both races and conformed more closely to the letter of the law. The Government assembled no less than 5,325 exhibits to demonstrate discrimination. The district court was persuaded insofar as the evidence related to the activities of the earlier board of registrars. The decision noted that:

> ... the previous Board did not carry out its obligations impartially. In fact, its members did not carry out their obligations according to law ...
>
> Between January, 1952 and December, 1960, ... the registrars registered approximately 4,500 white persons and only 88 Negroes. Only 14 Negroes were registered by the Board between June, 1954 and December, 1960.
>
> Between January 1, 1952 and December, 1960 the defendant State of Alabama, and its agents, the registrars of voters in Dallas County, refused to register many qualified Negroes and registered many white applicants who are not qualified.

However, the Court held that all of this was water over the dam. The new board was not only acting lawfully but "has fulfilled its duties in a manner which could well be emulated by all other boards in the United States." The Government was told that it should not seek injunctions against practices which have been discontinued and are not likely to be resumed.

[87]*U.S. v. Atkins*, 210 F. Supp. 441 (1962).

The Government appealed, focusing its argument on all the Negroes rejected and all the illiterate whites illegally registered during the period 1952 through 1960. The Attorney General held, in effect, that the county had already registered practically all of its adult whites, literate and otherwise. Now, with more Negroes seeking to register, the new board had suddenly discovered the merits of a high level of literacy and the desirability of strict adherence to the letter of the law. The Government insisted that the lower court should have complied with its request to "freeze" the standards actually applied to whites who had registered between 1952 and 1960.

The Court of Appeals conceded much validity to this argument, but they ruled that the use of this "freezing"

> should be invoked only when there is a great need for it. To apply the freezing idea too freely would mean that no state which had discriminated against Negro voting rights in the past could ever tighten its qualifications ... Moreover, when the application of this principle would mean that the Board must in the future continue to violate state laws as did its predecessors, the principle should be used, assuming such use could ever be justified, only if there were no other alternative by which justice could be reached.

Although the *Atkins* case raised an intellectually substantial question, the trend of judicial opinion has been to rule that the change to higher standards just as a record number of Negroes seek to register is a form of discrimination. *U.S. v. Duke*[88] is a landmark decision here. The Court of Appeals, overruling the district court in a case coming out of Panola County, Mississippi, noted that in the registration of whites there were "no standards." The decision posed this rhetorical question:

> Would anyone doubt the utter unfairness of permitting the unrestricted application by the State of the higher and stricter standards of eligibility to all of the Negroes in the County where 70 per cent of the white voters of the County

[88]332 F. 2d 729 (1964).

have qualified under simpler standards or no standards at all, and where the Negro citizens were prevented from qualifying under the simpler standards by reason of a practice or pattern of discrimination?

The same court, overruling the district court in *U.S. v. Mississippi and Wood*,[89] noted that in Walthall County whites had been registered on the basis of incredibly lax standards. The court was not persuaded as to the propriety of the county's sudden new zeal for high standards.

The discriminatory aspect of raising the standards was clearly enunciated by Judge Frank Johnson in *U.S. v. Parker*,[90] which was another stage in the lengthy litigation involving Montgomery County. On July 14, 1964, the Supreme Court of Alabama prescribed a new form for registrants. It required applicants to read and answer certain questions on government, to read from a section of the United States Constitution, and to copy excerpts from it. The contents of this new section of the application were changed each month. The Government asked the court to enjoin the use of this new material as violative of the injunction it had laid down in the *Penton* case. Judge Johnson was therefore talking in the context of earlier litigation when he said:

> The ... Board of Registrars' continued use of these different and more stringent standards results in discrimination against Negroes by "freezing" the white voters in the permanent status and "freezing" the Negro applicants out. The law is clear that where such illegal discrimination has worked inequality on a class of citizens and the court puts an end to such practice, but a new standard is adopted before the discriminated-against class may have the effect of their discrimination eradicated, the use of the new and more stringent standards is violative of 42 U.S.C. 1971 (a) and the 14th and 15th Amendments ...

Any remaining doubt as to the illegality of raising the standards in an area with a history of discrimination has been

[89]339 F. 2d 679 (1964).
[90]236 F. Supp. 511 (1964).

dispelled by a decision of a three-judge federal district court which was subsequently upheld by the Supreme Court. In *U.S. v. Louisiana et al.*[91] the Government made a frontal attack on the constitutionality of Louisiana's anti-Negro-voting legislation. A series of objective, standardized citizenship tests administered to all prospective voters alike had been adopted by the State Board of Registrars in August, 1962, pursuant to a statute and constitutional amendment. The district court noted that while the new citizenship test called for remarkably high educational standards, it was not *per se* unconstitutional. However, in the 21 parishes practicing voting discrimination the court could not overlook its grandfather-clause effect since most white adults in these parishes are already registered and very few Negroes are. The Court therefore enjoined use of the tests unless the state should decide to have a complete re-registration of voters and apply the tests to all citizens alike. The State of Louisiana appealed to the United States Supreme Court, which upheld the district court in a unanimous decision.[92] This court was a little tart in its reference to the citizenship test: "This is not a test but a trap, sufficient to stop even the most brilliant man on his way to the voting booth." A state cannot raise its standards coincidentally with an upsurge of Negro interest in registration when whites have for years been registering on the basis of much lower standards.

REMEDIES

The remedy for disfranchisement is the equity decree. Let us recall that the basic theory of civil rights legislation has been to avoid criminal prosecution. No amendments have been made to that section of the 1957 Civil Rights Act which reads:

> Whenever any person has engaged or there is reasonable grounds to believe that any person is about to engage in

[91]225 F. Supp. 353 (1963).
[92]85 S. Ct. 817 (1965).

any act or practice which would deprive any other person
of any right . . . secured by subsection (a) or (b), the Attorney General may institute . . . a civil action or other proper
proceedings for preventive relief, including an application
for a permanent or temporary injunction, restraining order,
or other order.

Having heard a case, the judge must frame a decree intended
to relieve whatever discrimination he finds. The terms of
the legislation offer the judge little guidance. Therefore,
there is a considerable area of flexibility as to the type or
extent of relief that will be granted. If a judge is not persuaded by the Government's arguments and he rules that only
one of the Government's half dozen forms of alleged discrimination is valid, no very comprehensive decree is called for.

In theory, a court decree may accomplish two things. It
may forbid the continuance of specified discriminatory practices or it may seek to rectify past abuses. Obviously a single
decree may be directed toward both objectives. A decree
seeking to end discriminatory practices may not be entirely
prohibitory because judges frequently give registrars positive
instructions on how to conduct their business in the future.
Thus, a registrar may be ordered to call the attention of all
applicants to any omission in the application form that may
result in their disqualification. However, most of the decrees
are phrased in terms of prohibitions, and they are illustrated
by the lengthy list of discriminatory practices set forth in
the foregoing pages.

The mere fact that some kind of decree is rendered does
not necessarily facilitate Negro registration. Some decrees
with only future applicability may have the effect of strengthening recently enacted anti-Negro-voting legislation. Consider again the case of *U.S. v. Mississippi and Wood*.[93] Here,
indeed, District Judge Cox did rectify one past injustice; he
ordered the board to register Masie Bullock, a Negro woman,
within five days. Beyond this he confined himself to ordering

[93]VIII (1963) *RRLR* 1537.

the board not to register anyone unable to read and write and explain a properly selected section of the Mississippi Constitution, and the registrar was warned not to help anyone. The registrar was instructed to put 40 sections of the Mississippi Constitution in a jar and shake them up; applicants were to draw from the jar the section they had to read and explain. Discrimination in grading was prohibited. The only whites who could possibly be affected by this decree would be poorly educated young whites seeking to register as they became 21, whereas the ruling affected the entire adult Negro population. The 1960 census showed 4,536 whites of voting age in the county; a slightly larger number of whites were registered, due doubtless to failure to purge the registration rolls. Of the nearly 2,500 Negroes of voting age in the county, two were registered, and Masie Bullock made three. Whenever any of the 2,487 other adult Negroes attempted to register, they would have to meet higher standards. The point is that the judge's solemn injunction against any discrimination in grading or other treatment of applicants is, in this context, solemn nonsense. Yet it is more than nonsense; this kind of a decree helps maintain Negro disfranchisement.

The foregoing does not constitute original thinking; the Court of Appeals reached the same conclusion earlier.[94] Noting that Walthall County whites had been registered on the basis of incredibly lax standards, the court entered a freeze order: "Moreover, since the freeze order which will have to be entered by the trial court contemplates the temporary suspension of the state's statutes regarding registration . . ." The Court of Appeals was concerned with rectifying past injustices. It offered the trial court some guidance in framing a decree and suggested that the registrars concern themselves only with age, poll-tax payment, non-criminal record, and ability to read the application form. Employment of

[94]339 F. 2d 679 (1964).

the test on the Mississippi Constitution was specifically enjoined.

The kind of court decree that actually enfranchises some Negroes is the type designed to correct past injustices. The earliest instance of such use occurred in the Macon County case. In this case, decided on March 17, 1961, District Judge Frank Johnson enjoined a number of discriminatory practices and issued to the board of registrars specific instructions on how to conduct registration. In addition, he ordered the immediate registration of 64 Negroes who, he ruled, had been discriminated against in the past. When the case was appealed,[95] the State of Alabama confined its argument largely to a contention that the judge had exceeded his authority in ordering their immediate registration. The Circuit Court upheld Judge Johnson. They called attention to the part of the Civil Rights Act of 1957 empowering the Attorney General to institute ". . . a civil action or other proper proceedings for preventive relief, including an application for a permanent or temporary injunction, restraining order, *or other order.*" Moreover, the Court noted that subsection (d) uses strong or mandatory language in prescribing that the district court "*shall* have jurisdiction" on such proceedings and "*shall* exercise the same without regard to exhaustion of administrative or other remedies . . ." The Court placed considerable emphasis upon the language "or other order." They ruled that this grants considerable option and flexibility to the district judge. Moreover, the Court relied on traditional equity concepts. "In prescribing a suit to be brought by the sovereign for equitable relief, the statute contemplates that the full and elastic resources of the traditional court of equity will be available to vindicate the fundamental constitutional rights to be secured by the statute."

Judge Johnson developed the idea further in layman's language in the Montgomery County case.[96] He explained

[95]*State of Alabama v. U.S.*, 304 F. 2d 583 (1962).
[96]*U.S. v. Penton*, 212 F. Supp. 193 (1962).

that his decree had three objectives: first, to correct partially past injustices; second, to forbid the continuation of discriminatory practices; third, to establish actual "qualification standards" and insist that the board observe in the future the standards it had been applying in the past. The first objective was achieved by ordering the immediate registration of 1,070 Negroes who had been the victims of double standards. Establishing actual "qualification standards" means discovering the standards that the board has applied to white applicants they have accepted and then insisting that they continue to use these toward Negro applicants in the future. Only this insistence that the actual "qualification standards" be observed prevents the grandfather-clause effect.

Concern for eliminating the grandfather-clause effect may raise some anxiety as to whether a state can ever raise its standards. Judge Johnson has in at least two decisions contemplated or answered this question. His position implies that the restraint on raising standards is a temporary affair. In *U.S. v. Cartwright*[97] he enjoined the use of a form recently prescribed by the Supreme Court of Alabama, which provided for certain questions testing the applicant's "knowledge of government." After noting that these tests had not been taken by 95 per cent of the whites that the board had approved for registration since November, 1959, the judge ruled, "the State and the defendant Registrars may not now adopt new and more stringent registration requirements or standards, the effect of which is to perpetuate past discrimination—until the prior discrimination and the effect thereof have been eliminated." Judge Johnson used similar language concerning the same set of questions as they applied to Montgomery County:[98]

> The law is clear that where such illegal discrimination has worked inequality on a class of citizens and the Court puts an end to such practice, but a new standard is adopted

[97]230 F. Supp. 873 (1964).
[98]*U.S. v. Parker, et al.*, 236 F. Supp. 511 (1964).

before the discriminated-against class may have the effect
of their discrimination eradicated, the use of a new and
more stringent standard is violative of 42 USC 1971 (a) and
the 14th and 15th amendments . . .

Note in both decisions the concept of a time limit: "until
the prior discrimination and the effect thereof has been eliminated." The same concept appears in *U.S. v. Louisiana, et
al.*,[99] in which a three-judge district court enjoined, in 21
discriminating parishes, the use of a newly devised citizenship
test. After noting that the use of the test would have a grandfather-clause effect, since most white adults were already registered and few Negroes were, the court ruled, " . . . until the
discriminatory effect of the tests has been vitiated to the
Court's satisfaction, we enjoin the use of the tests." Here
again, the prohibition on raising standards is for a limited
time only.

Before leaving the subject of remedies, some attention
should be given to the subject of voting referees. In the
debate on the passage of the 1960 act, much attention and
dispute centered on the voting-referee provision. The law
provides that once a pattern or practice has been found by
a court, the judge may appoint a voting referee. To the referee,
who must be a qualified voter in the judicial district, is
delegated the authority to take testimony from any Negro
applicant who has been turned down since the finding of
the pattern or practice and who claims that he has been
turned down solely because of his race or color. The referee
then decides which applicants meet the standards of *state*
law, or such parts of state law as have not been enjoined,
and reports his findings to the judge, who thereupon gives
the registrars an opportunity to challenge the qualifications
of the Negroes on the referee's list. Unless the qualifications of
some of these applicants are successfully challenged, they
are registered forthwith. Presumably the intent of this pro-

[99]225 F. Supp. 353 (1963).

vision was to free the district judge from some detailed work. The referee is empowered to do nothing the judge cannot do himself, and the appointment of a referee is discretionary with the judge.

The referee provision has been unimportant in practice. Only one referee has actually been appointed, and the most far-reaching decrees have been handed down by judges acting without benefit of a referee. In the Macon County case the district judge explained his reasons for not appointing a referee:

> This Court, for the time being, declines the request of the United States that it appoint voting referees for Macon County, Alabama. Such a declination is made with the idea that defendants can act fairly if the directions spelled out in this Court's decrees are followed in good faith. If the defendants so act, they will have regained for Macon County and for the State of Alabama the integrity that the evidence of this case makes abundantly clear has been lost in this field of voting rights.

The Justice Department had every reason to be pleased with all other aspects of the court's decree and did not appeal this failure to appoint a registrar. Nor was a referee appointed in the lengthy litigation involving Montgomery County. Again, in the *Penton* case the Government had no reason to be disappointed with the court's far-reaching decree. In the *Parker* case, the next step in the Montgomery County litigation, the court applied the freeze rule in enjoining the application of the newer and higher standards. The court specifically declined to appoint a referee as requested ". . . even though the pattern or practice of discrimination has continued to exist since the issuance of the original injunction in this case . . . " The Attorney General got an effective ruling here; he had no reason to be disappointed at not getting a referee.

If the criterion of effectiveness of the referee idea is the increase in Negro registration, it has not been a dramatic success. Perry County, Alabama, is a rural black-belt county.

On August 27, 1962, the Government asked for an injunction against discrimination in registration and asked for a finding of a pattern or practice. The court acted promptly. Declining to rule officially on the existence of a pattern or practice, Judge Dan Thomas noted that "defendants have engaged in acts . . . which have had the purpose and effect of depriving Negroes of their right to register without distinction of race or color."[100] The court ordered the registrars to refrain from some half dozen discriminatory practices. On January 9, 1963, the Government asked that the Perry County registrars be held in civil contempt for failure to obey the injunction. This Judge Thomas declined to do, but gave the registrars even more specific instructions on what to do and what not to do and gave them 60 days to obey or show cause why they should not be cited for contempt.

Although Judge Thomas never articulated the exact words "pattern or practice," the next legal step assumed that he had in effect ruled this. Recall that once such a finding has been made ". . . any person of such race or color resident within the affected area shall . . . be entitled, upon his application therefor, to an order declaring him qualified to vote, upon proof that at any election or elections (1) he is qualified under State law to vote, and (2) he has since such finding by the court been (a) deprived of . . . the opportunity to register to vote . . . or (b) found not qualified to vote." Soon Judge Thomas had on his desk 173 "letters" from Negroes who alleged that they had been deprived of the opportunity to register or had been found not qualified to vote despite their possession of the necessary qualifications. Judge Thomas acted on 16 letters whose writers asserted that they had not been informed whether or not they had been accepted for registration. However, he rejected the majority of the letters on the grounds of their legal insufficiency. They lacked specific information and did not allege particular irregularities. Hence, the letters were not "applications."

---

[100]*U.S. v. Mayton,* VII (1962) *RRLR* 1136.

The Government appealed and won a favorable decision in a suit styled *U.S. v. Hon. Dan H. Thomas.*[101]   The Court of Appeals ruled that Judge Thomas had indeed found a pattern or practice even though he did not use these precise words.   They noted that the legislative history of the act indicated the words meant a finding of something other than an isolated act of discrimination.   The court continued by noting that once a pattern or practice had been declared, "Any person of such race . . . resident within the affected area shall . . . be entitled, upon his application therefor, to an order declaring him qualified to vote."   The legal issue then became: What is an application?   The Court of Appeals reasoned that the purpose of the 1960 law was to expedite and simplify in order to avoid the case-by-case procedure of the 1957 law.   Surely the intent was not to delay the process with arguments about the sufficiency of applications or to set up a new technical gauntlet filled with chances for inconsequential errors.   The fact that the act required a hearing within ten days on such an application shows that speedy procedure was expected.   The actual proof of discrimination is to be made at the hearing, not in the application.   Congress assumed ignorant laymen would apply; a layman need only tell the judge that he wants to become a voter but the state authorities will not let him.

The decision concluded in a tone that might have been applied by a senior executive who was mildly irked by a junior subordinate's inability to solve problems unaided.   It noted that matters of this nature were perplexing for an already overburdened judge but observed that able judges must exercise ingenuity.   A resourceful judge might develop a questionnaire-type petition, or he could appoint a referee.   The district judge took the second alternative and appointed as referee O.S. Burke, an attorney in Greensboro, a town of 3,000 and the county seat of neighboring Hale County.   Burke, appointed September 23, 1964, acted promptly.   The number

[101]335 F. 2d 153 (1964).

of applicants had increased somewhat while the case was on appeal. He recommended to the court that 24 applicants were qualified and should be registered; he rejected 185 for various reasons, *e.g.*, 60 were already registered, 13 failed to appear before the referee, etc.[102] The activity of a referee is continuous once appointed. Thus, Referee Burke did not cease to be a referee after processing this batch of applications. As other Negroes in Perry County were denied registration on what they believed were racial grounds, they were entitled to bring their case to Referee Burke's attention. Early in February, 1965, the Birmingham *Post Herald* reported that Burke had recommended that seven more voter applicants be placed on the rolls in Perry County, thus increasing to 33 the number recommended by Burke. In this same period he had turned down a total of 224 other applications.

Apparently the jurisdiction of a referee is coterminus with that of the district court. Whenever any county in that judicial district is found to have engaged in a pattern or practice of discrimination, appeal may be taken to the same referee. Another Alabama newspaper[103] reported that 31 Dallas County Negroes had applied to Referee Burke after having been rejected by that county's board of registrars on February 15. Of these, 23 were ruled qualified and placed on the voting rolls.

FRONTAL ASSAULTS

Persons disposed to right the world's wrongs without undue delay may find this case-by-case, county-by-county approach unbearably slow. Everybody knows, it may be argued, that the state constitutions of Louisiana, Mississippi, and Alabama, as well as many of their laws, are intended to disfranchise Negroes. Why, then, assume that these are constitutional laws merely being applied in an unconstitutional fashion by county registrars? Why not make a frontal attack on all

[102]*U.S. v. Blackburn*, IX (1964) *RRLR* 1338.
[103]*Tuscaloosa News*, April 24, 1965.

laws and constitutions that are intended to disfranchise?
Then one can get at the root of the trouble.

The Department of Justice was persuaded to this approach
and brought suit on this theory in all three states. On January
15, 1965, it brought suit against the State of Alabama, asking
that the difficult new voter application test be enjoined. This
test was prescribed by the Alabama Supreme Court on January 14, 1964, and revised in August of that year. The Government's contention was that this raising of standards had
the effect of freezing the present racial imbalance among
Alabama's voters. The case never came to trial and was
rendered moot by the enactment of the Voting Rights Act
of 1965.

The frontal assault on Louisiana disfranchising devices
occurred in *U.S. v. Louisiana, et al.*[104] Under attack as violative of the Fourteenth and Fifteenth Amendments were the
State's constitutional-interpretation requirements and the more
recently enacted citizenship tests. The Louisiana Constitution
of 1921 requires that before a person registers he must "be
able to understand and give a reasonable interpretation of
any section of either constitution (National or State) when
read to him by the registrar . . ." A statute uses almost the
same language: "Applicants for registration shall be able
to read any clause in the Constitution of Louisiana or the
United States and give a reasonable interpretation thereof."
The citizenship test is an objective test enacted in 1962.

A three-judge district court was convened to hear the case.
The court ruled in favor of the Government by a two-to-one
majority. The constitutional-interpretation test was ruled
invalid *per se;* it could not possibly be administered in a
constitutional fashion. The decision, written by Circuit Judge
John Minor Wisdom, is a remarkably able treatise on political
history. He holds that the purpose and motive of the interpretation test is rooted in the historic determination to main-

[104]225 F. Supp. 353 (1963).

tain white supremacy in state and local government. While
the purpose of the Constitutional Convention of 1898 was
to safeguard white supremacy, he notes that even that gather-
ing specifically rejected a proposal for an understanding clause
as too obviously a fraud and adopted instead a grandfather
clause as an alternative to a literacy and property qualification. Then in 1915 the U.S. Supreme Court outlawed the
Oklahoma grandfather clause. To plug this loophole, Louisiana called a constitutional convention in 1921. Its sessions
were secret and no minutes were kept, but the delegates
substituted for the grandfather clause the understanding test
which had been rejected a generation earlier. However,
this test was rarely, if ever, applied until the early 1950's
when the demise of the white primary brought a rise in
Negro applicants for registration. There follows a remarkably complete story of the organization of the Citizens
Councils and the Joint Legislative Committee. These or-
ganizations—one private, one governmental—cooperated on a
two-step program: purge the registration rolls of great numbers of Negroes on the theory that they are unqualified voters
who have been illegally registered and, secondly, apply the
interpretation tests strictly to all new applicants for registration. There follows a detailed description of how the tests
were used in a discriminatory fashion after 30 years of disuse.

Concerning the objective citizenship tests, the decision
noted that they called for remarkably high educational standards but were not *per se* unconstitutional. In most Louisiana
parishes there is no alleged discrimination in registration.
However, in the 21 parishes where voting discrimination exists,
the use of the tests would have a grandfather-clause effect
since most white adults are already registered and few
Negroes are. Unless there is a general re-registration in
these 21 parishes (although this is not ordered) or until the
discriminatory effects of the tests have been vitiated to the
Court's satisfaction, the use of the tests is enjoined. A unan-

imous decision of the U.S. Supreme Court upheld Judge Wisdom's decision in all respects.[105]

United States v. Mississippi[106] was the Government's major effort to demolish Mississippi's 1962 package of election laws and certain earlier legal provisions. The United States brought an action naming as defendants the State of Mississippi, members of the State Board of Election Commissioners, and six county registrars of voters. The Government sought a declaration that certain provisions of the Mississippi Constitution are unconstitutional on their face and in their applications to Negro citizens. A special three-judge district court ruled against the Government by a two-to-one majority.

The decision is lengthy and the reasoning finespun. The decision did not really handle the substantive issues of the case. Instead the suit was dismissed on the ground that the Government failed to state any claim on which relief could be granted. In more popular language, the district court held that the Government had not named as defendant any entity that could be sued. The decision held that: the Civil Rights Act of 1960 authorizes suits against a state only when there are no voting registrars in office as was for a time true of Macon County, Alabama; secondly, there were doubts about the constitutionality of the act anyway if it authorized suits against states in their "sovereign entities"; thirdly, the State Election Commission was not a proper defendant because it did not appoint registrars; and, finally, individual registrars cannot be sued jointly for their separate, individual acts. Although the real burden of the decision was that the Government had not named a suable defendant, the court did have something to say on constitutional issues. It asserted that "There is no provision in the Constitution or a statute of Mississippi which deprives any person of the right to vote because of race or color." The admittedly exacting procedures and requirements are legal because they

[105]85 S. Ct. 817 (1965).
[106]229 F. Supp. 925 (1964).

apply to all unregistered voters—a complete rejection of the freeze theory. The Government's presentation of statistics was ruled immaterial because state laws apply equally to all persons.

The U.S. Supreme Court unanimously rejected this line of reasoning in *U.S., Appellant v. Mississippi, et al.,*[107] decided March 8, 1965. A brief decision rejected the idea that the Government had not named a proper defendant and remanded the case to the lower court for trial on its merits. "The case should have been tried. It should be tried without delay."

[107]380 U.S. 128 (1965).

III

Problems of Enforcement

THE PRECEDING CHAPTER was planned as a static presentation—an exposition of what the law is. The plan for a static presentation was a failure. The real message of the chapter, forcing itself up through the lengthy description of cases, was that the Justice Department was confronted with a rugged task in enforcing the law. Arrayed against it was the whole subculture of the Deep South. The first line of defense was the local official—the registrar and the attorneys, local and state, that represented him. Behind the local officials stood the state legislatures and the federal judges, not all of the latter being believers in Negro enfranchisement. There was nothing complex about the role of a legislature elected by a segregationist majority. Its members know that segregation and Negro disfranchisement is right. When a state law or constitutional provision is struck down as violative of one of the civil rights acts, this is perceived as the unwillingness of the federal courts to "leave us alone to manage our purely local affairs." Any right-thinking legislator will vote to enact a new statute or propose a constitutional amendment designed to circumvent or nullify the decision. It becomes a game between the Department of Justice and the legislature. Even when the legislature loses, it gains time—it postpones the evil day. It may take the Department another 18 months to knock down the new legislation. Unlike federal judges who experience some role conflict (as will be explained below), legislatures are merely playing their expected role of battlers for segregation. Since a description of their activities is easier, let us turn to it first.

LEGISLATIVE GAMESMANSHIP

Much of this legislation has been described earlier. The only value of touching on it again is to add a time dimension and to give a feeling of the interaction between courts and legislature. Let us begin with the Mississippi story. This is of value partly because it shows the Mississippi Legislature taking alarm at the march of events even prior to the passage of the Civil Rights Act of 1957. The Mississippi Constitution of 1890, Section 244, provides:

> ... Any Elector shall ... be able to read any section of the constitution of this State; or he shall be able to understand the same when read to him, or give a reasonable interpretation thereof.

Note that the section permits an applicant to vote if he is able to meet any one of three alternative requirements, namely—read, understand, or interpret. Apparently some time in the late 1940's or early 1950's, when a few Negroes began to show an interest in registration, the practice developed of requiring Negro applicants not only to read, but also to interpret, sections of the state constitution. This practice was challenged, and in 1951 the United States Court of Appeals in *Peay v. Cox*[1] pointed out that Mississippi registrars were violating the state constitution since it permitted people to vote if they could meet any one of the three requirements. The sequence of events from here out are well

[1]190 F. 2d 123 (1951).

described in *Voting in Mississippi: A Report of the U.S. Commission on Civil Rights, 1965:*

> The following year the Legislature proposed to legalize the practice questioned in the *Peay v. Cox* case by amending Section 244 to require all applicants to read and interpret any section of the Constitution. This proposal was rejected in a referendum in the November, 1952, election.
>
> The Legislature met next in 1954, during a period of heightened racial feeling following the Supreme Court's school desegregation decision. It again adopted a resolution to amend Section 244 similar to the one rejected in 1952. This time the resolution also required the applicant to demonstrate "a reasonable understanding of the duties and obligations of citizenship under a constitutional form of government."[2]

Note that no new registration was required. The new requirements were to have no effect on persons registered before January 1, 1954, that is, most white adults and very few Negroes. This is the familiar tactic of raising the standards when it appears likely that Negroes may register. This time the amendment was ratified by the electorate.

In 1960 the state constitution was amended again. The new provision read:

> In addition to all other qualifications required of a person to be entitled to register for the purpose of becoming a qualified elector, such persons shall be of good moral character.[3]

No legal standard to measure good moral character was provided. Presumably a county registrar had unlimited discretion. Also in 1960 the legislature passed a statute[4] repealing the requirement that application forms be retained as permanent records and adopted a new rule that, save for some technical exceptions, registrars need no longer keep

[2]Pp. 4-6.
[3]Section 241-A.
[4]*Mississippi Code Annotated*, #3209.6 (1962 Cumulative Supplement).

any record concerning registration. In short, registrars were free to destroy the evidence of discrimination. The same legislature enacted a group of statutes[5] making it unlawful to make false statements to any representatives of any branch of the federal government and specifically any representative of the FBI or the Civil Rights Commission. "It shall not be necessary to prove . . . that the oath or matter sworn to was material," one of the statutes says.

On April 10, 1962 the Department of Justice won a victory in the Court of Appeals in the protracted case of *U.S. v. Lynd*.[6] The court issued a temporary injunction directing the registrar of Forrest County to assist Negro applicants as he had previously assisted whites, to ignore insignificant errors and omissions in Negroes' forms, and to cease requiring that each unsuccessful Negro applicant wait six months before reapplying. The decision was given wide publicity in Mississippi, and the legislature reacted promptly. One week after the decision was handed down, bills were introduced: (1) requiring that application forms provide that applicants demonstrate their "good moral character" and that registrars observe this requirement; (2) strengthening the existing requirements that applicants fill in all blanks in the application form "properly and responsively" (meaning in a letter-perfect fashion) without any assistance; (3) directing the registrar not to advise rejected applicants of the reason for their rejection (except those rejected on account of bad moral character) "as to do so may constitute assistance to the applicant on another application"; (4) establishing a requirement that names of applicants for registration be published in a local newspaper once a week for two weeks as an invitation for voters to challenge the qualifications of the applicants. All four bills were all enacted into law the following month.

[5]*Mississippi Code Annotated*, #2155.4, 2155.5, and 2155.6.
[6]301 F. 2d 818 (1962).

This seems an almost classic example of what might be called "gamesmanship." The Department of Justice, after frustration in the district court and ultimate victory in the Court of Appeals, secured a modest decree from that court. The court acted, but the Mississippi Legislature reacted. Within less than two months it had enacted a package of laws designed to nullify the court's decision.

The Alabama Legislature also reacted. In 1951, Section 181 of the state constitution had been amended to require that each applicant complete

> a written questionnarie . . . the form and contents of which questionnaire shall be prescribed by the Supreme Court of Alabama. . . , which questionnaire shall be so worded that the answers thereto will place before the Boards of Registrars information necessary or proper to aid them to pass upon the qualifications of each applicant.

The Supreme Court produced a lengthy document containing 21 questions. Although one question required the applicant to "name some of the duties and obligations of citizenship," it was not otherwise an information-about-government test. In 1961 the legislature enacted the following statute:

> Section 1. On request of the Chief Justice of the Supreme Court of Alabama, the Legislative Reference Service shall prepare for consideration and approval by the Supreme Court at least 12 sets of questions, of such form and content as the Court may approve so that a different questionnaire may be filed by the Court with the Secretary of State . . . once each month for use by the several boards of registrars during the ensuing month.[7]

Apparently copies of the questionnaire circulated about the state, and some applicants were coached on the kinds of answers acceptable to their local boards.

The Chief Justice appears to have made no immediate request for additional questions, but the legislature was not

7Act No. 92, Regular Session of the 1961 Legislature.

idle. In the special session of 1961 the legislature passed Act 21, a proposed amendment to the state constitution, and Act 320, a lengthy enabling act. Taken together they attempted to set up a state board of examiners for voter registration. Act 459 required a prospective voter to pass

> ... a written examination which demonstrates his ability to read and write, in English any article of the Constitution of the United States, or any section of the Constitution or statutes of Alabama and his knowledge of the duties and obligations of citizenship under the statutes of the State of Alabama. Applicants for registration shall also be examined as to their knowledge of the duties and responsibilities and authority of state officers who are elected by vote of the people, and as to such other related matters as may serve to demonstrate their understanding of state government. No person may take the examination provided herein more than once during any calendar year.

The examination was to be prepared by "or in behalf of" the State Board of Examiners for Voter Registration. In each county the county board of registrars would give to an applicant a sealed envelope containing his examination. The act provided further that:

> The examination shall be uniform in all cases, with no discrimination between applicants ... except that the board shall construct new examinations, from time to time, so that no person may pass the examination simply by memorizing the answers to a specific set of questions.

Upon completing the examination, the applicant was to seal the answers in another envelope addressed to the State Board of Examiners. Each examination was identified by number only, and the grading of each examination was to be done at the state level, not at the county courthouse. The language of the proposed amendment was studded with numerous expressions such as "regardless of race, creed or color." In May, 1962, the Alabama voters rejected the proposed amendment. The new legislature, elected in 1962, met in the spring of 1963 and passed Act 417, the same proposed constitutional amendment that the voters had turned down less than a year earlier. The language of the proposed amendment and that of Act 459, the enabling act, was identical with that of the earlier laws save for the addition of a sentence providing that the intelligence level required of voters must not be below that required of members of the armed services. In December, 1963, the voters of Alabama again rejected the amendment.

In January, 1964, the Alabama Supreme Court at long last exercised the power granted to it in 1961. The Court's order[8] provided the 12 sets of questions—one for each month—authorized by the 1961 statute. Each set of questions was divided into two parts. In the first part the applicant had to answer a four-question information test. Questions dealt with such matters as the number of states in the United States, the capital city of the United States, the capital city of Alabama, the number of U.S. Senators per state, etc. The second section of the test contained excerpts from the U.S. Constitution which the applicant had to read aloud. Thereafter the registrar dictated to the applicant several words from that constitutional passage to comply with the state court's order: "the board members shall have the applicant write several words . . . to make a judicial determination of his ability to write." In Dallas County it meant in practice that

> the applicant had to demonstrate his ability to spell and to understand by writing individual words from the dictation of the registrar. Applicants in Selma were required to spell such difficult and technical words as "emolument," "capitation," "impeachment," "apportionment," and "despotism."[9]

[8]The Court's order is reproduced in full in the appendix of *U.S. v. Parker*, 236 F. Supp. 511 (1964).
[9]Testimony of Attorney General Katzenbach before the Senate Committee on the Judiciary, *Hearings, Voting Rights*, 89th Congress, 1st Session, 1965, p. 11.

After passage of the Civil Rights Act of 1964, which required that all tests be wholly in writing, the requirements of reading aloud and responding to dictation were dropped. The State Supreme Court then substituted for it by an order of August 26, 1964, 100 short-answer, knowledge-of-government tests. They were gathered in book form, and the applicant would select one test by turning to a particular page at random. The registrar would then give this written test to the applicant.

The actions of the Louisiana Legislature have been described earlier and need only be summarized here. The Constitution of 1921 contained an understanding clause which was rarely, if ever, applied until the upsurge of Negro registration in the early 1950's. Following the school desegregation decision, the Association of Citizens Councils of Louisiana became very active in insisting that the interpretation test be given to Negro applicants. This was especially true in the 21 parishes of the northern part of the state. The test was used very effectively in the customary double-standard fashion. In 1962 the State Legislature passed Act No. 62 which required the State Board of Registration to prepare, and order the local registrars of voters to apply, an "objective test of citizenship under a Republican form of government." A constitutional amendment to the same effect was adopted at the general election on November 6, 1962. Apparently this was a knowledge-of-government test and administered in a non-discriminatory fashion—that is, non-discriminatory save that the majority of the adult white population had registered on the basis of lower standards. Probably the motivations of the new tests were best stated by Court of Appeals Judge John Minor Wisdom when he observed in *United States v. Louisiana*:[10]

> By resolution of August 3, 1962, in compliance with Act 62 of 1962, the State Board of Registration adopted a voter-qualification test, apparently to fit this case should the interpretation test be held unconstitutional.

[10]225 F. Supp. 353 (1963).

The reference to "this case" refers to *U.S. v. Louisiana*, the case which Judge Wisdom was deciding. The state legislature wanted to be prepared for an adverse decision.

THE SEGREGATIONIST JUDGE

A more formidable obstacle than hostile legislatures to making the civil rights laws effective was the segregationist judge. A federal judge in the South was a white southern politician before he became a judge. He had grown up with a set of values and loyalties before becoming a jurist called upon to enforce federal laws that often clashed with these values. No suggestion is intended that a judge is so crude as to say to himself when he writes a decision, "I'll fix these damn interfering Feds and their fool laws." Yet there is a clash between the role of a judge as a member of the federal court hierarchy and his southern background. An axiom of civil rights legislation has been to avoid criminal proceedings. Keep the litigation civil and avoid the segregationist jury which might applaud and acquit the violator of federal law. Yet if southern juries may have a segregationist bias, does elevating a southern white lawyer to a federal district judgeship (he must reside in the state where he serves) free him from all the values and loyalties with which he grew up? His personality was formed in a society that segregated everything from maternity wards to cemeteries. In addition to these internal controls are the external controls. He may risk ostracism if he renders decisions in harmony with federal law but offensive to his white neighbors. His very kinfolk in Greensboro, Greenwood, and Greenville will shake their heads sadly in disbelief when he "rules in favor of the niggers."[11] And we must recall that the reliance on equity proceedings accentuates the importance of judicial bias. Even in cases

[11]This parallels the line of argument of Jack Peltason in his *Fifty-eight Lonely Men: Southern Federal Judges and School Desegregation* (New York: Harcourt, Brace, 1961).

where the evidence is so preponderant that a judge must rule in favor of the Government, he may still hand down a decree so mild that it makes little change in the situation.

One may reasonably inquire whether a judge could not have an integrationist bias. We might recall that the Civil Rights Acts of 1957, 1960, and 1964 were intended to remove obstacles to Negro voting; their language made the intent of Congress reasonably clear. The statutes were designed to enforce the Fifteenth Amendment and to produce more Negro voters. Hence, if a judge enforces the law, there is no way of telling whether he does so reluctantly or with an enthusiasm based on his social philosophy.

This begs the question of what is the yardstick for judicial bias. The first criterion is a judge's *dicta*. Some jurists do not confine themselves to the immediate issue nor limit themselves to the use of colorless language. Consider these expressions found in various decisions: stirring up distrust between the races; alien intruder; people of the Southland; agitators who do not understand . . . There can be no doubt about the loyalties of such jurists. There is a certain quaintness about their forthrightness, a certain obliviousness to the larger world. A second criterion is useful for judges who do not convict themselves out of their own mouths. This is a little primitive judicial score-keeping. If a judge's record on Negro voting cases is 7-0 against the Government, we have a *prima facie* case that he is not a champion of the Fifteenth Amendment; and if these decisions cover points of law on which some of his colleagues have ruled differently, it is hard to explain his rulings on any ground other than bias. It is worth noting that one district judge has shown in an opinion a sensitivity to the charge of bias.

A few segregationist judges identify themselves. In the course of a decision such a judge frees himself from the narrow confines of the law and expounds his social and political philosophy. No other jurist could approach the late Circuit Judge Ben Cameron in this respect. His finest effort was his dissent in *U.S. v. Wood, et al.*[12] It will be recalled that this case involved the young Tennessee Negro who conducted a registration school in Walthall County, Mississippi. When he brought two of his students into the county courthouse, Registrar Wood took out his pistol and struck him on the back of the head, saying, "Get out of here you damn son of a bitch and don't come back in here." As Mr. Hardy stood in front of the courthouse bleeding from a scalp wound, the sheriff arrested him for disturbing the peace. The Justice Department saw in this a baseless arrest— a misuse of state criminal procedure to intimidate registration organizers. A majority of the Court of Appeals was persuaded that this looked suspiciously like a case of intimidation and issued a temporary restraining order. Judge Cameron dissented. After devoting some time to the novel legal issue of enjoining a state from continuing with a criminal prosecution, he turned to a lengthy statement of his political philosophy and his view of the role of a federal judge in the South. He began with some unflattering comments about John Hardy: ". . . based largely on the statements made by a person of palpable irresponsibility who had come from a distant point to the State of Mississippi to stir up distrust between the races." The "distant point" was neither New York nor Boston but Nashville, Tennessee. Evidence of Hardy's irresponsibility is a quotation from a newspaper interview in which Hardy avows atheism and a disbelief in service in the armed forces. Judge Cameron continued:

> It is . . . a saddening spectacle to witness . . . decisions such as that of the majority here, which can have no other effect than to cause the people of the southland to look upon federal functionaries . . . , as "alien intruders."

Judge Cameron then said that he was constrained to repeat the language he has used in a recent dissent. This language, with some deletions, follows:

[12]295 F. 2d 772 (1961).

It is the universal conviction of the people of the [South] also that the judges who function in this circuit should render justice in individual cases against a background of, and as interpreters of, the ethos of the people whose servants they are.

He went on to observe that the judges were selected in a manner following "normal political lines" and that only residents of a particular judicial circuit were eligible for appointment to judgeships in it. Then he continued:

It is the firm conviction of the [people of the South] also that decisions such as this one, in cases brought by or on behalf of Negroes and involving the equal protection clause of the Fourteenth Amendment, have not been in harmony with the spirit, thought and desires of the people, the vast majority of whom, in both races, know that their common problems can best be worked out if they are left alone to continue the unbroken improvement in relationships which has taken place in the last eight decades. They are keenly conscious of the fact that since the end of the tragic era following the War Between the States . . . there has been a continuing growth in mutual understanding, respect and brotherhood between the members of the two races; . . .

The rank and file of Negroes, resent the efforts of the agitators who do not understand, to [throw into the courts matters of status and relationships which can best be worked out in the friendly atmosphere of close community contacts].[13] They feel . . . that the judges should perform their duties with a sympathetic understanding of the true facts; and further that such an understanding has been tragically lacking in many of the decisions of many of the Judges of the Fifth Circuit whose actions have gone so far to the other extreme that *Time Magazine* gave six of the Judges an enthusiastic write-up with photographs in its issue of December 5, 1960 . . . The article, . . . was headed "Trail-Blazers on the Bench—South's U.S. Judges Lead a Civil Rights Offensive." It stated that the Judges extolled constituted "an honor roll without precedent in United States

---

[13]Brackets supplied by Judge Cameron. Recall that he is quoting an earlier dissent of his own.

legal annals" and that they had "collectively . . . launched one
of the great, orderly offensives of legal history."

This is not the time . . . to set neighbor against neighbor—
to adopt a course which will . . . lead to the destruction of
the . . . understanding necessary to the continued advancement
. . . of both races.

It is unthinkable that a handful of agitators . . . would
be permitted to interrupt that advance and set the stage
for another "Tragic Era."

He expressed similar sentiments in writing the majority
opinion in *U.S. v. Mississippi*.[14] His peroration began:

After having importuned this Court to strike down sub-
stantially all which the people and the legislature have written
during the tedious, sometimes tragic, years in which they
have endeavored to maintain a government of laws, [the
Justice Department] . . .

Since Judge Cameron's death in 1964, no jurist has revealed
his sympathies so clearly and with so little effort to obscure
them in legal jargon. Daniel H. Thomas, Judge of the Southern District of Alabama, occasionally employs in his decisions
language that reveals his values. *U.S. v. Atkins*[15] was the case
in which Judge Thomas distinguished carefully between a
previous board of registrars which "did not carry out its obligations impartially. In fact, its members did not carry
out their obligations according to law," and a new board
which was acting legally and was unlikely to resume the illegal practices of its predecessors. After observing that ". . .
the present board had fulfilled its duties in a manner which
could well be emulated by all other boards in the United
States," he continued:

In approaching my duty in this case, I do so with the knowledge that there is a terrific sociological problem involved.
Dallas County, Alabama, has problems which other sections

14229 F. Supp. 925 (1964).
15210 F. Supp. 441 (1962).

do not have. They have problems that other sections do have but do not admit because of political expediency. These problems must be resolved and should be resolved by the people and not by the courts. To the credit of the Dallas County Board of Registrars, they have fairly resolved this most important problem.

Judge Thomas ignored the fact that Congress had recently enacted two laws commanding that this particular sociological problem be resolved through the courts and giving judges specific responsibilities concerning its resolution.

The Hon. E. Gordon West, Judge of the District Court for Eastern Louisiana, has ruled on only three voting-rights cases. An indication of his racial attitude may be inferred from his opinion in *Davis v. East Baton Rouge Parish School Board*.[16] Judge West introduced his decision with these remarks:

> I could not, in good conscience, pass upon this matter today without first making it clear, for the record, that I personally regard the 1954 holding of the U.S. Supreme Court in the now famous *Brown* case as one of the truly regrettable decisions of all times. Its substitution of so-called "sociological principles" for sound legal reasoning was almost unbelievable. As far as I can determine, its only real accomplishment to date has been to bring discontent and chaos to many previously peaceful communities, without bringing any real attendant benefits to anyone.
>
> And even more regrettable to me is the fact that almost without exception the trouble that has directly resulted from this decision in other communities has been brought about not by the citizens and residents involved, but by the agitation of outsiders, from far distant states, who, after creating turmoil and strife in one locality, are ready to move on to meddle in the affairs of others elsewhere.

Let us note quickly the three voting-rights cases heard by Judge West. He was the dissenter on the three-judge district

[16]214 F. Supp. 624 (1963).

court that invalidated two fundamental features of Louisiana's voting laws in *U.S. v. Louisiana,* the majority opinion later being upheld by the U.S. Supreme Court. In *U.S. v. Palmer*[17] and *U.S. v. Harvey*[18] the registrars of two Louisiana parishes closed their offices completely after the district court's decision in *U.S. v. Louisiana.* The registrars contended they were caught between federal and state law. The Government asked Judge West to order the registration offices to be opened immediately and petitioned him to forbid certain forms of discrimination. He forbade discrimination, as asked by the Government, but declined to order the registrars to open their offices and expressed some sympathy for the difficult position of the registrars caught between state law and what he referred to as the opinion of a "divided court." He prohibited discrimination by registrars whose offices he allowed to remain closed.

Most judges refrain from overt expressions of praise for segregation. If a judge does not wear his prejudices on his sleeve, how can we demonstrate their existence? The procedure here will be to summarize quickly the decisions of those district judges whose decisions have been least sympathetic to Negro voting rights. The procedure will involve a very primitive type of scorekeeping, stated in terms of decisions for or against the Government. This arithmetic must be handled with some reservation. These are not strictly "for" or "against" decisions. The Government may secure injunctive relief but of a weaker and less far-reaching type than requested. Or a judge who has been ruling consistently against the Justice Department may tamely parrot a Court of Appeals ruling only after an obviously irritated appellate judge has laid down the law so clearly that the district judge no longer has room to maneuver. Yet to credit a judge with a pro-Negro decision in this case would be misleading. Also an effort will be made to compare the decisions

[17]230 F. Supp. 716 (1964).
[18]IX (1964) *RRLR* 780.

with those of some of their judicial colleagues who have ruled differently on the same points of law or shown a greater willingness to take judicial notice of obvious facts. Surely Justice Department attorneys must be behavioralists at least to this extent; they must know in advance whether they are pleading before a friendly or a hostile judge. And at least one judge registers some consciousness of the possibility of his being classified as a segregationist judge. Ben Dawkins, Jr., Federal District Judge of Western Louisiana, ruled against the Government in *U.S. v. Lucky.*[19] Toward the end of his opinion he took occasion to note:

> This court has not hesitated, in appropriate cases, to issue injunctions against Registrars of Voters because of unlawful discrimination. See, e.g., [six such cases are listed]. Here, however, we must find . . .

Is not the jurist saying, in effect, "Look, fellows, I am not ruling against you because I am a segregationist. I have decided in your favor six times; today you just don't have a good case." If a judge thinks in terms of his batting average, it lends support to an analyst thinking in the same terms.[20]

Judge William Harold Cox of the Southern District of Mississippi, a one-time roommate of Senator Eastland at Ole Miss,[21] is entitled to high priority in any discussion of segregationist judges. He rendered thirteen voting rights decisions. He ruled against the Government in ten of these cases, in its favor in two, and rendered one ambiguous decision. Judge Cox's most amazing case was *U.S. v. Lynd.*[22] The complex legal aspects were well summarized in the decision of the Court of Appeals in overruling him. *U.S. v. Lynd* is, strictly

---

[19]239 F. Supp. 233 (1965).

[20]Lest it be felt that the author is not a sufficiently zealous quantifier, let it be noted that most studies of jurimetrics have applied simple yardsticks like pro- or anti-something, or they have dealt with a multi-member court like the U.S. Supreme Court. The behavior of nine judges all voting on the same cases readily lends itself to scale analysis.

[21]*Time,* March 5, 1965.

[22]301 F. 2d 818 (1962).

speaking, the name of an appeals case culminating a series of actions in the lower court. The case began with the Government's plea that Registrar Lynd of Forrest County, Mississippi, had not permitted a single Negro to register. He rejected no whites and even aided them in filling out their forms. The action began with a get-the-records struggle. On August 11, 1960, the Government requested Lynd to make available his records. He did not comply. On January 19, 1961, the Government sued in Judge Cox's court for enforcement of its request. Six months elapsed during which the judge did not act. On July 6, 1961, although the Government never secured access to the records, it nonetheless asked the Court to enjoin Lynd from further discriminatory practices. Judge Cox took no further action until February 15, 1962, when he dismissed the enforcement proceedings, i.e., the requests for the records, as "abandoned" on the grounds that the second suit superseded it. On March 5-7, 1962, the case was tried on its merits. Judge Cox, having denied the Government access to the records, now insisted that the Government prove its allegations in great detail. The defense declined to offer any evidence at this time but asked for 30 days to prepare answers; Judge Cox granted the request. The Government asked for a temporary injunction; the judge neither granted nor refused the injunction but did grant the 30-day recess.

The only two cases in which Judge Cox ruled unequivocally for the Government were *In re Coleman*[23] and *In re Gordon*.[24] Yet here is an instance where arithmetic can be misleading. *U.S. v. Lynd* was followed by *Kennedy v. Lynd*.[25] *U.S. v. Lynd*, which was consolidated with *Kennedy v. Bryce* and junction favorable to the Government but did not touch on the get-the-records aspect. This aspect was handled in *Kennedy v. Lynd*, which was consolidated with *Kennedy v. Bryce* and three other Louisiana cases. The Court of Appeals admin-

23208 F. Supp. 199 (1962).
24218 F. Supp. 826 (1963).
25306 F. 2d 222 (1962).

istered Judge Cox nothing short of a tongue-lashing. The decision included this sharp language:

> After a series of motions, motions to dismiss, opposing substitute motions for more definite statements . . . but no clearcut ruling, no indication that this interminable proceeding would ever come to an end, . . the District Court effectually denied the Attorney General's application.

The decision continued, "on its merit, the action is clearly wrong." After a lecture on the meaning of Title III of the 1960 Civil Rights Act the Court concluded, "There is nothing left to dispute . . . and the District Court is directed to grant without further delay the application to have these records made available . . . as requested." Judge Cox did indeed rule in favor of the Government in the *Coleman* and the *Gordon* cases; with this harsh language ringing in his ears, he could scarcely have done otherwise.

Kennedy v. Owen[26] is based on the fact that in Mississippi the country registrar is also the circuit clerk. Attorney General Kennedy had sent a records-inspection demand to the registrars of seven Mississippi counties, addressing each of them as circuit clerk. Judge Cox thereupon granted to the Attorney General an inspection order to examine the records each defendant possessed in his capacity as circuit clerk but not those possessed in his capacity as registrar of voters. The Court of Appeals did not regard this as a legitimate technicality and noted that the federal statute referred to the "demand by the Attorney General to the person having custody, possession, or control of such record or paper." The demand had to be made to the person having custody of records. Possession of records alone was important; addressing the custodian by his exact title is unimportant.

In *U.S. v. Daniel,* Judge Cox refused the Government's request for an injunction to restrain further racial discrimination in Jefferson Davis County, Mississippi. The injunction

[26]321 F. 2d 116 (1963).

was refused because the registrar on the stand "invited . . . instructions from the court and [promised] that he would immediately and voluntarily comply with such instructions in every detail." The judge further justified the refusal in order "to avoid the stigma of any appearance of government by injunction . . ." When a national law specifically provides for injunctive relief, it is difficult to see why the issuance of such an injunction involves any stigma.

U.S. v. Green is another example of Judge Cox's reluctance to move vigorously in this area. In this case,[27] the Government contended that Registrar Green used more stringent standards toward Negroes than he did in registering whites. The Government asked that Green be restrained from a continuation of these double standards and that six Negroes who had been the victims of the double standards be registered forthwith. Judge Cox went halfway with the Justice Department. He was persuaded by the Government's pleading that the "plaintiff is entitled to a restraining order." The court ordered Green in the future to register all applicants in the same manner. Yet Judge Cox declined to order the registration of even six Negroes. The Court agreed that discrimination had been practiced, but it declined to rectify past injustices. This could be compared with the decisions of Judge Johnson in the cases involving Montgomery, Macon, and Bullock Counties in Alabama. Here, impressive numbers of Negroes against whom the local registrars had practiced discrimination were ordered registered by the judge. Nor was Judge Cox willing to find that a pattern or practice of discrimination existed. Had such a finding been made, the Justice Department could have requested the appointment of a referee, who might have expedited registration.

U.S. v. Ramsey[28] involved eight Negroes who were denied registration by the registrar of Clarke County, Mississippi. They were told to go home and think it over whether they

27*New York Times,* April 22, 1962.
28VIII (1963) *RRLR* 156.

really wanted to register. Three Negroes in the county were already registered; so was the entire adult white population, including large numbers of illiterates, some of whom were registered without even appearing at the office. Judge Cox agreed that the eight Negroes had been discriminated against but ruled that no pattern of anti-Negro discrimination had been demonstrated. The registration of illiterate whites was due entirely to the inefficient manner in which the 82-year-old registrar ran his office.

Judge Cox was even more emphatic in his refusal to find a pattern or practice in *U.S. v. Mississippi and Wood*.[29] He ruled that there was no doubt that Wood, the registrar in Walthall County, Mississippi, had discriminated against the few Negroes who had applied. He had given them hard sections of the state constitution to read; white applicants were given easy sections. The Government attempted to demonstrate a pattern on the basis of registration figures. The white registration consisted of somewhat more than the 4,536 whites of voting age enumerated by the 1960 census takers. Of the 2,490 Negroes of voting age, only two were registered. These figures did not persuade Judge Cox. He ruled:

> Such statistics are thus misleading and completely distort the facts insofar as the issues of this case are concerned. Such imbalance in registration is occasioned solely by reason of the fact that Negroes have not been interested in registering to vote and very few have even bothered to apply to register prior to 1957; whereas white people have been intensely interested in voting in elections in that county.

Other district judges have held that statistics speak and judges listen. The Court of Appeals overruled Judge Cox in both the *Ramsey* and the *Wood* cases.

Nor has Judge Cox been disposed to find instances of intimidation. It will be recalled that the case of *U.S. v. Edwards*

29VIII (1963) *RRLR* 1537.

involved the Government's request for an injunction against any further intimidation of prospective Negro voters by Sheriff Edwards. The sheriff and his deputy had beaten three Negroes who were seeking to register in the courthouse. Judge Cox denied the request for an injunction. Conceding that the attack was deplorable, he ruled that it was an isolated event, not part of an official policy of Negro disfranchisement. *U.S. v. Holmes County*[30] presents some involved facts but appears to be a case in which the victims of harassment were arrested by local officials. As mentioned earlier, a fire bomb was tossed into the home of a Negro who was acting as a host for an out-of-town civil rights leader. The leader, Robert Moses, was charged with complicity of arson and impeding the investigation of the fire by the sheriff. The Justice Department sought an injunction against any further harassment of civil rights workers by Sheriff Smith. Judge Cox refused to issue an injunction because he felt that there could be no relation between the fire and Moses' voter registration campaign because no local people of either race were interested in it. Judge Cox did note that Sheriff Smith had refused to accept poll tax payment from Negroes, and he was ordered to desist from this practice.

Nor was Judge Cox any more disposed to issue an injunction against intimidation in the case of *U.S. v. Wood, et al.* This case, which produced Judge Cameron's colorful dissent on appeal, was the one in which the Negro who had been conducting a registration school was driven out of the Walthall County courthouse by Registrar Wood, who struck him on the back of the head with his pistol. Although the victim of the attack was arrested for disturbing the peace, the judge declined an injunction on the ground that the issue "does not involve a controlling question of law." Judge Cox was unwilling to see in these actions the misuse of the state's criminal procedure to deny a person a right protected by federal law.

---

[30]IX (1964) *RRLR* 229.

Again, in *U.S. v. Ashford,*[31] Judge Cox ruled against the Government, and the facts, mentioned earlier, are well worth repeating. Mr. Ashford, the registrar of Hinds County, close his registration books on the ground that he was swamped preparing for the 1963 primary election. The Justice Department asked Judge Cox for an injunction setting aside the state court order. The Department submitted the following facts. Of the 70,000 registered voters in Hinds County, only 5,000 were Negro. A Negro registration drive was in progress at the time the registrar closed his office. Between June 12 and July 5, some 700 Negroes tried to register but found facilities lacking. When on July 3 the state court heard Ashford's request for an injunction, neither the Department of Justice nor the county's citizens were given an opportunity to be heard. The Government noted that in the past the registrar's office had been capable of processing over 100 applications a day and emphasized that Mississippi law does not permit the closing of the registrar's office prior to elections. The suit further alleged that at the time the 700 Negroes unsuccessfully attempted to register, 129 whites applied and 124 of these were accepted. A layman unlearned in the law might have suspected an effort to frustrate the Negro registration drive, but Judge Cox held the "closing of the books non-discriminatory."

In view of Judge Cox's reluctance to see violations of federal law in these varied factual situations, one would hardly expect to see him vote to invalidate a whole package of Mississippi election laws and parts of the state constitution. Yet this is what the Government asked in *U.S. v. Mississippi.*[32] This was the case in which the Government abandoned its county-by-county approach and launched a frontal attack on Mississippi's election laws. The nature of the case required the calling of a special three-judge district court. It consisted of Court of Appeals Justices Cameron and Brown and District

[31]*New York Times,* July 14, 1963, p. 48.
[32]229 F. Supp. 925 (1964).

Judge Cox. Once the personnel of the court was determined the Justice Department must certainly have known how the case would be decided. Justice Cameron, who had proclaimed that it was his role to interpret the Constitution in harmony with the "ethos of the people of Mississippi," would hardly be expected to rule that Mississippi had been unlawfully disfranchising its Negro citizens throughout the preceding 75 years. Nor could any sane person expect that Judge Cox, whose lack of enthusiasm for Negro voting had been demonstrated in the dozen cases set forth above, would strike down all of Mississippi's disfranchising provisions. The judges split two-to-one. Justice Cameron spoke for the majority, writing a lengthy opinion. Judge Cox concurred and also contributed a concurring opinion. The Attorney General had about as much chance of winning in that court as Nasser would have of being elected mayor of Tel Aviv.

Claude F. Clayton, the judge of the Northern District of Mississippi, appears to have handled only three cases in this area. Judge Clayton has a perfect record of ruling against the Government—three to nothing. His decisions have been characterized by a narrow and highly technical interpretation of voting rights legislation. Consider his handling of *Kennedy v. Lewis*.[33] This was a demand by the Attorney General for the records in the custody of the registrar of Bolivar County, Mississippi, in pursuance of the provisions of the Civil Rights Act of 1960. Judge Clayton did, indeed, issue an injunction, but he severely limited the papers that could be examined. The Government could examine only papers pertaining to the primary and general elections of 1960 and the records of the *eligible* voters. These restrictions denied access to the records of would-be voters who might have been illegally disfranchised. The Court of Appeals overruled him.[34] This was a remarkable decision because all the issues involved

[33]IX (1964) *RRLR* 227.
[34]325 F. 2d 210 (1963).

had been settled earlier in *Kennedy v. Lynd*,[35] which made clear that the Attorney General was to have access to *all* records.

This same proclivity toward technicalities also appeared in *U.S. v. Dogan*.[36] Here the Attorney General sought an injunction requiring the sheriff of Tallahatchie County, Mississippi, to permit Negroes to pay their poll taxes and asking the judge to find that a pattern or practice of discrimination existed. Judge Clayton began by ruling that the case be limited strictly to the term of the present sheriff, who had served for only a few years. Thus, evidence of discrimination prior to Sheriff Dogan's term was ruled inadmissible. Since only two Negroes had attempted to pay their poll taxes during Dogan's term, this was held to be inadequate evidence of a pattern of discrimination. Moreover, the judge did not find that there had been discrimination against even these two. Judge Clayton explains how one arranges to pay poll tax in Tallahatchie County:

> ... the deputy was then to obtain from the applicant information as to the age, residence, and voting precinct of the applicant and advise the applicant either to take the matter up with the Sheriff personally, or to come back in a few days within which time the deputy would present the matter to the sheriff for his determination.

Judge Clayton, apparently in all seriousness, puts poll tax payment on the same level of complexity as securing a license for a new television station from the Federal Communications Commission. The two Negroes had not asked to see the sheriff personally or supplied the deputy with the information required by state law. "These efforts were superficial at best and did not . . . carry the hallmark of bona fide efforts in good faith to pay poll taxes." The judge was not persuaded by the fact that nearly all adult whites were registered and no Negroes were even permitted to pay a poll tax. The

---

[35]306 F. 2d 222 (1962).
[36]206 F. Supp. 446 (1962).

Court of Appeals overruled him,[37] holding that racial discrimination was being practiced up to the day of the trial and quoting approvingly from *Alabama v. U.S.*,[38] "In the problem of racial discrimination, statistics often tell much, and Courts listen."

In *U.S. v. Duke*,[39] Judge Clayton declined to find a pattern or practice in Panola County, Mississippi, despite the fact that the only Negro registered was a 92-year-old man who had registered in 1892. The judge ruled:

> The fact that not more than 20 Negroes have attempted to register since 1932 refutes completely the implications plaintiff draws erroneously from statistical data showing the number of qualified voters among the numbers of the white race in Panola County as compared with the number of voters among the Negro race.
>
> The evidence shows that Duke and his deputies . . . gave assistance to white persons applying for registration. There is no evidence that he refused to help any Negro. They simply did not ask for help.

The fact that many illiterate whites were registered did not prove a policy of discrimination. The judge attributed this to the work of inept, inexperienced deputy registrars. The Court of Appeals overruled him.[40] The Court held that the deputy registrars were not inexperienced but had had long experience. After listing four types of discrimination practiced by the registrar, the Court once again observed that "statistics often tell much, and Courts listen."

A discussion of the obstacles to the enforcement of voting rights legislation in Alabama must give some attention to Judge Daniel H. Thomas of the Southern District. Reference was made to Judge Thomas earlier as a jurist whose decisions contained political preaching. He cannot be classed in

[37]314 F. 2d 767 (1963).
[38]304 F. 2d 583 (1962).
[39]IX (1964) *RRLR* 788.
[40]332 F. 2d 759 (1964).

precisely the same bracket as Judges Cox and Clayton. An air of certainty pervades their decisions. Thomas, though usually segregationist, occasionally wavers and shows signs of doubt and confusion.

Judge Thomas went along with the fantastic series of delaying actions used by the Wilcox County registrars in their effort to keep the Attorney General from inspecting their records. The Court of Appeals[41] finally ruled in favor of the Attorney General and chided Judge Thomas with the statement ". . . we are unable to find any conceivable justification supporting the trial court's action." Judge Thomas dutifully ordered the Wilcox registrars to make their records available, but he was willing at a later date to continue the delaying action on a technical nicety. The Justice Department wanted some earlier records—those for the years 1952-1958. On October 17, 1962, Judge Thomas ruled that these earlier records were never in the "physical custody of the registrars" but were held by Circuit Solicitor McLeod. It was necessary for the Justice Department to return to court and institute a new suit naming a different defendant.

In *U.S. v. Logue*[42] Judge Thomas could find no fault with the voucher requirement (the device by which a registered voter must assure the registrar that an applicant is the person he asserts he is and not an imposter). Safeguards against impersonation seem unnecessary in a small rural county where, as the saying goes, everybody knows everybody else. In 1963 Wilcox County, 70 per cent Negro, experienced the novelty of 29 Negroes making applications to become voters. When all applicants were rejected for failure to secure a voucher, the Justice Department asked the Court to set aside the voucher requirement. Judge Thomas began by noting that the efforts to register were sparked "largely through the efforts of voter registration workers who were sent into Wilcox County." There had been only one instance

[41]*Kennedy v. Bruce*, 298 F. 2d 860 (1962).
[42]IX (1964) *RRLR* 770.

of a Negro asking a white person to vouch for him; the white refused. Ruled Judge Thomas, "It is the firm belief of this Court that a diligent effort on the part of any qualified Negro applicant would produce many registered voters who would vouch for him . . ." He distinguished between this case and the *Manning* and *Ward* cases in Louisiana because in these cases there had been "an intent" to discriminate. Here, everyone—black or white—was required to secure a voucher; hence there was no discrimination. The Court of Appeals[43] demolished this fragile reasoning. It observed that many whites testified that they did not know who filled out that part of the form nor did they request anyone to vouch for them. Sometimes the registrar suggested to the applicant the names of persons who might serve as a supporting witness. County officials vouched for 342 of 386 applications. No one suggested possible witnesses for Negroes, and none of their forms was signed by county employees. The Court likened the voucher in Wilcox County to the former requirement that an alumnus of the University of Mississippi recommend each student who applied for admission.

Rather more involved were the two Dallas County cases— *U.S. v. Majors* and *U.S. v. Atkins.* The trial was delayed some ten months while the Attorney General struggled to secure the voting records. Finally the Court held that although the records were in the custody of the grand jury, the defendant registrars were actually using them every day. It will be recalled that in this case Judge Thomas drew a distinction between the voter registrars that left office in December, 1960, and the board that followed them. Referring to the earlier board, Judge Thomas noted the registrars of voters in Dallas County refused to register many qualified Negroes and registered many white applicants who were not qualified. Yet ". . . the present board has fulfilled its functions in a manner which could well be emulated by all other boards in the United States." Since the present board was nondiscrim-

43344 F. 2d 290 (1965).

inatory, Judge Thomas saw no need for an injunction to rectify the injustices committed by the old board, whose "members did not carry out their obligations according to law." This is in marked contrast to the handling of the past-injustice problem by his brother jurist in the neighboring district, Judge Frank M. Johnson, Jr., in the cases involving Montgomery, Macon, and Bullock Counties. This contrast is further brought out in Judge Thomas's statement:

> "Well, there may be differences of opinion on many of these applications. There is a human element involved in the grading of any examination paper. One person has his or her own ideas as to how a paper should be graded. Another person ... may well have other ideas ..."

By this statement Judge Thomas abdicated any responsibility for seeing that the applications were evaluated in a nondiscriminatory fashion. When Judge Johnson handled this issue, he accepted responsibility for reading hundreds of application forms to see that there was no double standard.

The case of *U.S. v. Mayton* was a series of actions stretching over two years. On August 27, 1962, the Government filed a motion alleging discrimination in Perry County and requesting an injunction against its continuance and the finding of a pattern or practice. Judge Thomas heard the case with a minimum of delay, found that at least since 1959 defendants had been discriminated against, and issued a decree telling the registrars what to do and what practices to refrain from. However, he did not specifically find a pattern or practice. Judge Thomas seemed less sure of himself in subsequent stages of the litigation which resulted when the Perry County registrars did not hasten to comply with his orders. Largely at issue was the question of whether the judge had indeed found a pattern or practice, even though he did not articulate these precise words. The Court of Appeals[44] ruled that he had and that he must therefore act on the 173 letters sent

[44]335 F. 2d 153 (1964).

him by Negroes alleging denial of registration by the board, either through the appointment of a referee or otherwise. In this case the jurist started out vigorously but seemed to become less assured when the board did not comply with his orders and when he was in other respects confronted with an unprecedented situation.

In *U.S. v. Ford*,[45] Judge Thomas handled a suit arising out of Choctaw County. The suit was brought on June 15, 1962; it was tried on February 20, 1963; the decision was handed down on April 13, 1964. The facts were routine: 3,697 whites were registered and 176 Negroes. In the immediately preceding four years the defendant board of registrars had registered 782 whites and rejected only two; in the same time they registered 42 Negroes and rejected 260. A recent act of the Alabama Legislature had raised the standards required of prospective voters. Judge Thomas noted a number of discriminatory practices and issued a fairly vigorous decree, but his decree took no notice of the fact that most of the white adults of the county had become registered under less exacting requirements than were now to be applied to Negro applicants. In short, he declined to apply the freeze theory. This refusal should be compared with the decision of another federal judge with respect to another black-belt county, Sumter County. District Judge H. H. Grooms, who rendered the decision in *U.S. v. Hines*,[46] is not known as a racial liberal, yet he enjoined the registrars from using more stringent registration requirements than had been applied to whites since 1954. Judge Grooms noted:

> Where ... a great majority of one race is already permanently registered while but a small minority of the other race has succeeded in registering, the adoption and application of new and more stringent registration requirements or standards, the effect of which is to perpetuate past discriminations, are constitutionally impermissible.

[45]IX (1964) *RRLR* 1331.
[46]IX (1964) *RRLR* 1333.

The decisions, rendered only five months apart, dealt with rural black-belt counties. The legal issue was identical in each case. Yet Judge Thomas declined to take steps to insure that past discriminations not be perpetuated.

U.S. v. Bruce, it will be recalled, dealt with the Negro insurance salesman who was ordered to stay off the property of 28 landowners after he and his wife had led a registration drive. The Attorney General filed a complaint on December 20, 1963. Oral argument on the defendants' motion to dismiss the complaint was heard on April 7, 1964. On June 30, 1964, Judge Thomas granted the defendants' motion to dismiss. He gave no reason for the dismissal. Eighteen months later the Court of Appeals held this an instance of coercion and granted the relief sought.[47]

[47]353 F. 2d 474 (1965).

IV

Epilogue

THE EFFORT TO enforce the Fifteenth Amendment by means
of the judiciary was not a success story, at least not when
compared with the results produced by the Voting Rights
Act of 1965. The results of working through the judiciary
were summarized by Attorney General Katzenbach:

> What has been the effect of these statutes? It is easy to
> measure. In Alabama the number of Negroes registered to
> vote has increased by 5.2 [percentage points] between 1958
> and 1964—to a total of 19.4 per cent of those eligible by
> age and residence . . .
>
> In Mississippi, the number of Negroes registered to vote
> has increased at an even slower rate. In 1954, about 4.4
> per cent of the eligible Negroes were registered; today,
> we estimate the figure at about 6.4 per cent . . .
>
> And, in Louisiana, Negro registration has not increased at
> all, or if at all, imperceptibly. In 1956, 31.7 per cent of
> the eligible Negroes were registered. As of January 1, 1965,
> the per cent was 31.8.[1]

On the first anniversary of the enactment of the Voting Rights
Act of 1965, the estimated percentage of Alabama Negroes

[1]U.S., Congress, House, Committee on the Judiciary, *Hearings, Voting
Rights,* 89th Congress, 1st Session, 1965, p. 4.

of voting age who were registered was 51.5. The comparable figures for Louisiana and Mississippi were 47.2 per cent and 32.9 per cent.[2]

But the experiment with the judiciary was not a total loss. The Voting Rights Act of 1965 was tailored to avoid all the weaknesses of the earlier legislation. Its drafters had in mind all the frustrations encountered in attempting to enforce the earlier statutes. In this sense, the Voting Rights Act of 1965 was a direct descendant of the earlier legislation.

The new law will not be reproduced here. It is lengthy and not the kind of lucid prose that would gladden the heart of an English teacher. Suffice it to say that all the frustrating obstacles have been swept aside. Biased judges cease to trouble; under the new law the courts have no role. Legislative gamesmanship is out; state voting requirements are frozen as they stood November 1, 1964. And you can prove discrimination by statistics!

A basic feature of the new act is its statistical formula to define discrimination. You do not have to bring a particular county official to trial and persuade a judge concerning his misconduct. Instead, the law recognizes what everyone knows, namely, that several states and many counties in the Deep South have long been violating the Fifteenth Amendment. According to the formula, a state or county is held to be practicing discrimination if *both* of these requirements are met: (1) Less than 50 per cent of the voting-age population were registered on November 1, 1964 or voted in the presidential election of that year, and (2) any "test or device" is required of prospective voters. The phrase "test or device" is defined to mean

> . . . any requirement that a person as a prerequisite for voting or registration for voting: (1) demonstrate the ability to read, write, understand, or interpret any matter, (2) demon-

---

[2]These figures come from the press release of the Voter Education Project of the Southern Regional Council. Release dated August 5, 1966.

strate any educational achievement or his knowledge of any particular subject, (3) possess good moral character or (4) prove his qualification by the voucher of registered voters or members of any other class.

Only when less than half of the adults in a test-or-device area are registered does the formula apply. Thus, New York, with more than half its adult population registered, can retain its literacy test. Texas, which employs no test or device, is unaffected by the act even though less than half of its adult population voted in November, 1964. The Attorney General determines the existence of the test or device; the Director of the Census certifies the percentage of voting-age persons registered. No court action is necessary; moreover, the above findings "shall not be reviewable in any court." Upon publication in the *Federal Register* of the names of states or counties affected by the formula, their tests or devices are automatically suspended. Applicants for registration appear before the usual local officials, who continue to enforce other state voting requirements such as age, length of residence in the state, American citizenship, etc.

The appointment of federal examiners occurs only in those counties where local officals refuse to comply with the law or do not expand their facilities and working hours to accommodate the masses of new Negro applicants. The Attorney General has almost unlimited discretion as to where registrars are to be sent. By early June, 1967, federal examiners had been sent to a total of 60 counties. Thirteen are in Alabama, four in Georgia, nine in Louisiana, 32 in Mississippi, and two in South Carolina.[3] The federal examiners register anyone who complies with such legitimate state voting requirements as age, residence in the state, etc.

State legislatures may no longer seek to outwit or circumvent Congress and the federal courts. If a state's "test or devices" have been suspended, it cannot change its laws

[3]Department of Justice news release, June 3, 1967.

on voting without the specific approval of the District Court of the District of Columbia.

Much of the new law is a larger application of the "freeze theory" hammered out in the courts in such cases as *Duke, Dogan,* and *U.S. v. Louisiana.* The freeze theory brought up the question whether a state could ever legitimately tighten its voting requirements. The courts answered this question by saying that the freeze was for a limited period of time only; new applicants (meaning, primarily, Negro applicants) were to be registered on the basis of the same indulgent standards or absence of standards that had prevailed for the white population. A limited period of time was necessary to erase the effects of earlier discrimination. At the end of this period the state would be free to raise its voting standards. The new law incorporates this idea. Literacy tests or other devices are suspended for a period of five years. At the end of five years a state's chief legal officer may appear before the District Court of the District of Columbia and seek to persuade that body that the effects of past discrimination have been eradicated. If he is successful in this endeavor, the tests or other devices may be reinstated, and the state can alter its voting laws in other respects.

There is some risk of concluding with too broad a generalization. Critics of the Voting Rights Act of 1965 express outrage over the fact that "illiterates are permitted to vote." In many areas of the Deep South—particularly Alabama, Mississippi, and Louisiana—voting has been treated as a right that belongs to a white person when he reaches maturity. While there have been exceptions, "tests and devices" have not been serious obstacles to poorly educated whites. The effect of the new legislation is to permit poorly educated Negroes to register and vote just like poorly educated whites.

Table of Cases

Index